PCS AND DIGITAL CELLULAR TECHNOLOGIES:

Assessing Your Options

PCS AND DIGITAL CELLULAR TECHNOLOGIES

Assessing Your Options

Rifaat A. Dayem

To join a Prentice Hall PTR Internet mailing list, point to
http://www.prehnhall.com/register

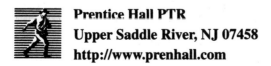

Prentice Hall PTR
Upper Saddle River, NJ 07458
http://www.prenhall.com

Editorial/production supervision: *Mary Sudul*
Cover design: *Design Source*
Cover art: *Tom Post*
Cover design director: *Jerry Votta*
Manufacturing manager: *Alexis R. Heydt*
Acquisitions editor: *Mary Franz*
Editorial assistant: *Noreen Regina*

 ©1997 Prentice Hall PTR
Prentice-Hall, Inc.
A Simon & Schuster Company
Upper Saddle River, New Jersey 07458

Printed in the United States of America
10 9 8 7 6 5 4 3 2 1

ISBN 0-13-616574-5

Prentice-Hall International (UK) Limited, *London*
Prentice-Hall of Australia Pty. Limited, *Sydney*
Prentice-Hall Canada Inc., *Toronto*
Prentice-Hall Hispanoamericana, S.A., *Mexico*
Prentice-Hall of India Private Limited, *New Delhi*
Prentice-Hall of Japan, Inc., *Tokyo*
Simon & Schuster Asia Pte. Ltd., *Singapore*
Editora Prentice-Hall do Brasil, Ltda., *Rio de Janeiro*

to Linda, Jennifer, Michael, Gabriel, and Leigh

Contents

Chapter 6.   Mobile Radio Systems   133

Chapter 7.   Conclusions   143

Bibliography   161

Appendix A.   Wireless Networking Applications   163

Preface

I have had the pleasure of leading seminars on my favorite subject, Wireless Networking in the United States, Europe, and Asia over the past four years. I have greatly enjoyed meeting and interacting with all those seminar attendees who are now helping shape this exciting new industry. I began dreaming about this kind of "magically connected" world three decades ago when I started working at Bell Labs. After more than 10 years there that included work on private voice and data networks and a PhD in microwave radio, I could not resist the lure of California, Stanford, and the budding Apple Computer. It was there that I had the opportunity to start working in this exciting field and watch it unfolding. This unfolding will not be a sudden change, but rather a steady emergence of new ways of connecting with each other and with the information we crave. I am very happy to be part of this unfolding, and honored to be able to share with you the insights in this book and in the companion book, *Mobile Data and Wireless LANs.*

Cellular communications is the most important telecommunications development since the introduction of the switched network. Cordless telephony and future Personal Communications Systems promise mobile communications to the mass market at affordable prices. This book provides valuable information on the evolution of cellular radio and its relationship to emerging Personal Communications Systems. In this book you will learn:

- Cellular and PCS market dynamics
- Radio propagation principles, fading, multipath, and intersymbol interference
- Modulation techniques including a critical comparison of TDMA and CDMA
- U.S. Digital Cellular and Japanese Digital Cellular
- GSM/DCS capabilities, technologies, and inner workings
- Cordless telephony and PCS: CT-X, DECT, PHS, and high-tier and low-tier PCS
- Mobile radio: PMR, PAMR, SMR, and ESMR
- Satellite services: GEO, MEO, LEO, and HEO.

The current wireless revolution is led by the spread of digital cellular (in particular, GSM) throughout the world. This will lead to future Personal Communications Systems (PCS) of all types. The first chapter is an overview of the cellular and PCS markets. To understand all the activities that are occurring throughout the world in the field of Wireless Networking, we present several "maps." The first map is based on where we spend our time, and organizes the evolution of products and services, the standards, and the spectrum allocations that are taking place in the

United States, Europe, Asia, and other parts of the world. A second map shows the types of user traffic and how well different wireless technologies serve them. A third map plots all the wireless services on a matrix of cell size and achievable data rate. With this overview, we present the market dynamics of analog cellular, digital cellular, cordless telephony, high-tier PCS, and low-tier PCS. To put the material in this book in perspective, a brief discussion of Mobile Data and Wireless LANs is included in this first chapter. The companion book entitled *Mobile Data and Wireless LANs* covers these areas in detail.

Wireless services are mostly carried in the microwave radio band. Designing an efficient and reliable system in this band hinges upon a good understanding of how signals propagate in this medium, the impairments of the signal due to fading and multipath, and ways of dealing with them. The available frequency spectrum is shared among its users through frequency, time, and code-division multiple access. How do these techniques compare? Which is the most effective for which service? What is the performance of each technique?

In the second chapter, we discuss radio propagation principles including Rayleigh fading, multipath, intersymbol interference, and ways of dealing with these impairments. We discuss modulation techniques including Frequency Shift Keying, Phase Shift Keying, Gaussian Shift Keying, and others. We present the various kinds of signal coding techniques ranging from error correction and coding to voice coding techniques. We talk about the two duplexing methods: Frequency Division Duplexing and Time Division Duplexing and in which systems they best apply. We then focus on multiple access alternatives, in particular, Frequency Division Multiple Access, Time Division Multiple Access, and Code Division Multiple Access. We give a CDMA example and provide insight on the controversial CDMA/TDMA debate. Finally, in this second chapter, we summarize the essence of cellularization principles.

Analog cellular has been serving mobile professionals for a number of years. The ramp in demand brought about the evolution to digital cellular. In the third chapter, first we present the background of analog cellular including Advanced Mobile Phone System (AMPS), Nordic Mobile Telephone (NMT), and Total Access Communications System (TACS). Then we discuss and compare the major digital cellular technologies, in particular, United States Digital TDMA (IS 54 and IS 136), Global System Mobile and Digital Communications System (GSM and DCS), and Personal Digital Cellular (PDC). Lastly, we summarize the basic satellite communications systems including: Geostationary Earth Orbit (GEO), Low Earth Orbit (LEO), and Medium Earth Orbit (MEO). We then consider how they fit in with cellular.

GSM/DCS 1800 is an important international standard, as it is the leading digital cellular standard being implemented throughout the world. Its first appearance in the United States is in the form of DCS 1900, which is one of the PCS standards we will discuss in Chap. 5. In the fourth chapter, we focus on the capabilities and inner workings of GSM/DCS. We begin with the objectives of GSM as stated in the standard, and the services it provides including voice services, Short Message Service (SMS), data services, fax services, supplementary services, the Subscriber Identity Module (SIM), and the GSM security functions. We then detail the functional architecture of GSM including operation and maintenance management, call management, mobility management, and radio resource management. Next, we present the GSM signaling systems that support establishing and releasing a call, call progress indication, handover management, special feature management, and Short Message Service transmission. Then we delve into the technology of GSM in the areas of speech coding, modulation scheme, frame formats, and cellularization design. Finally, we summarize GSM security functions for authentication and for provision of information privacy.

Aimed at lower cost applications and smaller areas of coverage, cordless telephony will be a complement to digital cellular and will provide higher density islands of coverage. Early cordless telephony systems will grow into future PCS systems. In the fifth chapter, we start with existing analog cordless phones that we find in almost every home in the United States and in many homes in Japan, Europe, and other parts of the world as well. Next, we turn to digital cordless systems covering CT-2 and variations, Digital European Cordless Telephone (DECT), Wireless PBXs, and Personal Handyphone in Japan. Then, we focus on Personal Communications Systems in the United States: Frequency allocations and the seven standards are considered. Throughout the chapter there are numerous comparisons of cordless and PCS systems, and comparisons of these systems with cellular systems. In the conclusion of Chap.5, we present a summary of future third-generation systems, namely, Future Public Land Mobile Telecommunications System (FPLMTS), and Universal Mobile Telecommunications System (UMTS).

The market for mobile radio is in the process of structural change from a private systems market to one that mixes the supply of private systems with the provision of public services. In the sixth chapter, we detail applications of Private Mobile Radio (PMR) and Public Access Mobile Radio (PAMR) and how they relate to cellular. We outline the relationship of PMR and PAMR systems with Specialized Mobile Radio (SMR) and Enhance Specialized Mobile Radio systems (ESMR). We present the major mobile radio technologies for private small, medium, and large systems, as well as for public systems. We discuss the Digital Short Range Radio (DSRR) standard for PMR systems and the Tetra standard for PAMR systems, and finally, summarize the supply chain for mobile radio systems.

I would like to express my deep gratitude to my loved ones for their encouragement and support with this pleasurable but sometimes preoccupying project. And, I would like to express my great appreciation to the many participants in the seminars that I have led in different parts of the world for their gracious input and feedback. I look forward to continuing to work with all of you who share the dream in this stimulating world of Wireless Networking.

Rifaat A. Dayem

1

The PCS and Cellular Markets

The current wireless revolution is led by the spread of digital cellular systems throughout the world. This will lead to future Personal Communications Systems of all types. In this chapter, we present:

- A wireless map showing the activities of Wireless Networking in the areas of
  - Cellular radio, cordless telephony, and PCS
  - Mobile data
  - Wireless LANs
- The radio spectrum
- Traffic types and technologies
- Cell size and achievable throughput
- Market forecasts
  - Analog cellular
  - Digital cellular
  - Cordless telephony
  - High-tier PCS
  - Low-tier PCS

A Wireless Map

There are a great many activities all over the world in the Wireless Networking field. In this section, we present a map to help understand the relationships among the activities. The map is based on where we spend our time. On this simple taxonomy we overlay the spectrum and standards activities worldwide, and the evolution of wireless products and services. We then present a vision that is very simple to state, but after seeing the complexity of the present situation, is not so easy to achieve.

The areas where we could be spending our time are shown in Figure 1.1. As illustrated, we could be in the office, in our home, or at a public area such as a shopping mall or a downtown area, or somewhere in between, for example, in our car, on a plane, or perhaps on vacation.

These possibilities are organized in the simple picture in Figure 1.2.

Most offices today are served by both a Local Area Network and a PBX. Local Area Networks were introduced in the 1970s to serve the needs of bursty traffic of very short duration. PBXs made an attempt at serving this kind of traffic but were not completely successful with the switching technology available at the time. PBXs used circuit switches and provided connection-oriented services that were aimed at voice traffic. It took a circuit switch of that era about one sec-

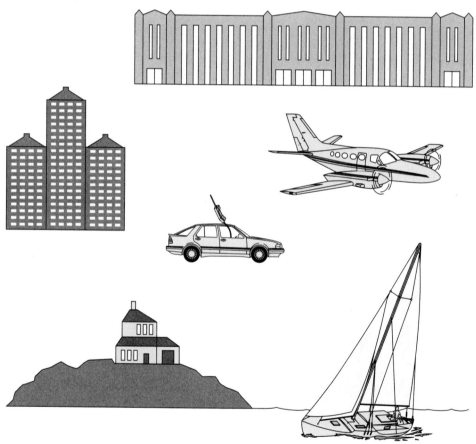

Figure 1.1   Where we spend our time.

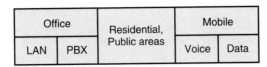

Figure 1.2   A taxonomy of where we spend our time.

ond to set up a connection. The message length for bursty traffic was about 50 milliseconds on the average. It was not economical to use a circuit switch that took one second to set up a connection for transmitting a message that lasted only 50 milliseconds. In addition, the response time was unacceptable. For these reasons, most offices installed a LAN to handle the bursty traffic, and a PBX for voice. The PBX was used for data as well—usually the data that were destined to locations outside the office campus. The PBX has thus served as the gateway to the wide area network.

Twenty-five years later, we now have the technology that will allow a single-switching fabric to meet the needs of bursty traffic as well as the needs of voice and other isochronous traffic that requires guaranteed bandwidth. This technology is Asynchronous Transfer Mode, or ATM. We are seeing LAN manufacturers use this technology to build high-speed LANs, and we are seeing PBX manufacturers use this technology to build future high performance PBXs. With ATM we will finally be able to have a single hub in the office to serve our data, voice, and other multimedia needs. Moreover, this hub will use the same technology as that used for wide area networks making the integration between the local area and the wide area seamless.

Will we see this same integration take place around ATM technology for Wireless Networks? Unfortunately, the answer to this question is: not in the near term. Wireless ATM is in its infancy at this time. There is much research being done on the subject; however, the first set of standards for Wireless LANs will not be based on ATM, but rather on traditional LAN technologies.

In the second part of Figure 1.2, we include both residential and public areas. This is because, as we will see, both these applications are served by the same technology. When we are on the move, we can be communicating voice or data, and that is how the third part of the figure is divided.

The evolution of services and the spectrum and standards activities based on this simple taxonomy is shown in Figure 1.3.

Today, we have Wireless LAN products from several manufacturers. We also are beginning to see Wireless PBXs from several telephony manufacturers. We can expect to see just about all future PBXs having wireless capabilities in the not too distant future.

For residential and public areas, today we have a huge installed base of cordless phones, particularly in the United States and Japan. These phones are built to meet simple regulatory rules from the regulatory agencies in these countries, but do not meet any kind of interoperability standard. It is not so important for cordless phones to interoperate at this time since it is not a strong requirement for a user to obtain the base station from one vendor and the handset from another. The regulatory rules do aim at making the sets coexist without mutual interference. The end result is not always satisfactory today. We often can hear our neighbors on our cordless phones. Neverthe-

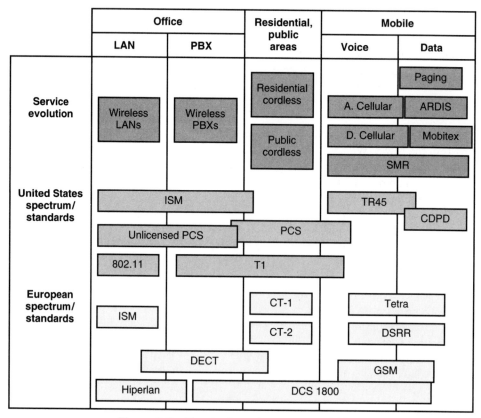

Figure 1.3 Standards and spectrum activities.

less, we buy these devices and use them willingly, because we like the freedom of not being tied to a cord in the wall. These cordless phones are the future roots of PCS. Their popularity shows that when the price and service are right, PCS will spread without bound. And this is indeed a long-term vision of PCS. It will essentially replace telephony.

Next, we have the mobile area. Here, analog cellular services provide voice services and some circuit-switched data services. Digital cellular provides voice and more data services. Paging provides mobile data service for alert-type traffic. Packet-switched networks such as those from Motorola and Ericsson provide mobile data for bursty type data traffic. The Motorola packet-switched networks have different names in different parts of the world. In the United States it is called ARDIS, in Europe it is called Modacom, and in parts of Asia it has different names such as Datatac. The Ericsson network is called Mobitex in most parts of the world. These two networks are competing for the customers whose applications have bursty traffic; both are racing to build networks. At the same time, two-way paging is beginning to be introduced by companies such as

SkyTel and Mtel. The packet-switched networks from Motorola and Ericsson will have to prove their price/performance advantage over the two-way paging networks.

Specialized Mobile Radio is perhaps the oldest kind of service shown on the chart. SMR services are the roots of Wireless Networking. They serve police departments, fire departments, ambulance drivers, taxicab companies, trucking fleets, airport operations staff, security services, and so on. All the walkie talkies and the one-way dispatch units we see in truck and cab fleets are based on SMR licenses.

Next, we discuss the spectrum and standards activities in the United States, Europe, and other parts of the world. Wireless LANs today have had to use the Industrial, Scientific, and Medical bands. To use the ISM bands, the products are forced to use complicated spread-spectrum technology as required by Part 15 of the FCC rules. Spread-spectrum is needed in order not to interfere with the primary users of this band. There are several ISM bands available. The most popular band that is available in many parts of the world including the United States, Europe, and parts of Asia is the 2.4 GHz ISM band. This is where most Wireless LAN manufacturers are aiming their initial products. The hope is that in the near future a band dedicated to this kind of traffic will be made available in most parts of the world. The first step has been taken in the United States with the provision of an unlicensed PCS band for asynchronous traffic. This 10-MHz band has been allocated by the FCC, but many implementation issues still remain before this band can be effectively used by the Wireless LAN industry.

A few manufacturers are using the ISM bands for other purposes. For example, Spectrix builds a wireless PBX that uses the ISM bands. Also, Metricom uses the ISM bands to provide what is essentially a wireless Metropolitan Area Network. Other uses of the ISM band abound. There are cordless phones that use the lower ISM band. These cordless phones provide much greater range, almost a mile, at about four or five times the price of an average cordless phone that barely covers a large house. The other half of the unlicensed PCS band is aimed at Isochronous traffic. This is the kind of traffic that requires guaranteed bandwidth such as voice and other multimedia traffic including video. Wireless PBX manufacturers are paving the way for effective use of this 10 MHz much faster than the Wireless LAN industry is able to do with the 10 MHz earmarked for asynchronous traffic.

The bulk of the spectrum for PCS is licensed and will be used for services aimed at the residential and the public area markets. In addition, it is possible that PCS will find its way into business systems, and some manufacturers are considering using PCS spectra to provide large scale mobility as is provided by cellular services.

The standards body that is responsible for Wireless LAN standards is IEEE 802.11. 802.11 products are likely to be provided throughout the world. PCS standards are developed by the T1 committee, as well as the TR45 committee. The T1 committee is a huge organization comprising more than 1,500 companies that are involved in all facets of communications equipment and services. Although its aim is the residential and public area markets, it has impact on the business market as well as the mobile market. The TR45 committee is involved primarily in developing cellular standards, and now it is involved in developing PCS standards as well. The TR45 committee issued the IS54 digital cellular TDMA standard, the later version of the digital cellular standard

IS136, the IS95 digital CDMA standard, and the IS41 interconnection standard. TR45 and T1 work together closely on projects such as PCS where they both have great interest.

Cellular Digital Packet Data is a standard that was developed by an industry consortium comprising IBM, six of the seven Regional Bill Operating Companies (RBOCs), and other major organizations. The aim of CDPD is to provide a packet data service for bursty traffic that is derived from the existing circuit-switched cellular services. It leverages the tremendous installed base of cellular base stations and switching equipment to provide a packet service. In essence this packet service provides additional revenues from the same infrastructure that is being used for voice traffic with relatively small additional investment.

Whereas the United States and Japan lead the market for cordless phones in the home, Europe and Asia lead the market in telepoint services. Telepoint service is cordless service in public areas. It can be thought of as a wireless pay phone. It is one-way outgoing and is provided in islands of high-density coverage. The standard used for these services at this time is CT-2. Initial telepoint services include Rabbit in the United Kingdom and Bibop in France; however, they seem to be declining in popularity. Their purpose seems to have been to serve as a learning step more than anything else. Even their names do not sound like they should be taken seriously. Their market position was not clear relative to GSM, and their penetration was too little to warrant further construction of the networks. In parts of Asia they enjoyed greater popularity, especially when combined with paging. However, even there they are beginning to wane, as they become replaced with GSM and other more mature PCS services.

Digital European Cordless Telephone was proposed by Ericsson as a wireless PBX standard. It is a mature standard that is implemented in chip sets by several manufacturers in Europe and in the United States. DECT has a good chance of becoming a worldwide standard for wireless PBXs. In addition, DECT can be applied in residences as a small cordless key set providing several handsets that are served by a single base station. DECT can also be used as a telepoint service replacing present CT-2 implementations if the market justifies it.

In the mobile data area there are two standards that have been developed by the European Telecommunications Standards Institute: Digital Short Range Radio and Tetra. DSRR is aimed at Private Mobile Radio, Tetra is aimed at Public Access Mobile Radio. There is not much activity with DSRR, but Tetra is being considered in all parts of the world. One of the keys to the success of the Tetra standard is how well it can meet the needs of closed user groups with stringent peak traffic requirements such as police departments, especially in times of emergency.

Finally, and most importantly is the GSM 900/DCS 1800 standard. The new name for GSM is Global System Mobile, and it seems to be living up to its name. It is the cellular digital standard with the widest acceptance throughout the world. However, it will not remain unchallenged as other digital cellular standards such as TDMA and CDMA reach maturity. GSM 900 provides larger cell applications than does DCS 1800. The power levels and the frequency of operation of GSM allow it to cover wider areas more easily than the lower power levels and higher frequency of operation DCS 1800.

In this book, we focus on the middle three columns of Figure 1.3. These are the areas that are served by telephony companies and cellular carriers. They provide wireless PBXs for on-site private system applications; in addition, they provide residential cordless systems for home use and public cordless systems for use in shopping malls, downtown areas, and other high-density areas. They provide cellular services for ubiquitous coverage wherever users are likely to be including roadways and rural areas.

Figure 1.4 shows Wireless Networking products and services relative to the taxonomy of where we spend our time.

There are Wireless LAN products from several vendors—some large, some very small. The large vendors include ATT, IBM, and Motorola. The small ones include Proxim, Xircom, and Spectrix. The Wireless LAN market is still in the start-up mode compared to the cellular market. It is difficult for a small company to remain viable in such a slow developing market. However, there is no question that eventually this market will develop as the price/performance formula becomes attractive.

The wireless PBX business is served by all the telephony manufacturers. A small sampling is shown in Figure 1.4. The same companies serve the residential and public areas market. Cellular carriers serve the mobile voice market. Paging and packet radio companies serve the mobile data market.

Now that we have seen all the Wireless Networking activities taking place around the world, we can discuss what the vision might be. Simply stated, one view is that Wireless Networking should be:

- Available everywhere
- Invisible to the user.

Office		Residential, public areas	Mobile	
LAN	**PBX**	**areas**	**Voice**	**Data**
ATT GIS		CT-X	ATT	Paging
IBM	ATT			
Proxim	NorTel		RBOCs	Ad. paging
Xircom	Ericsson	Ericsson		ARDIS
Motorola				
Windata	SpectraLink	NorTel	GTE, . . .	Mobitex
Photonics				
Spectrix		Hutchinson	McCaw	CDPD

Figure 1.4 Products and services.

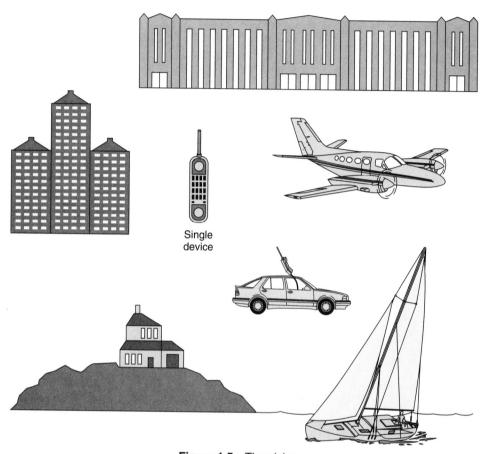

Figure 1.5 The vision.

This vision is very simple to state but is not so easy to achieve today. There are many different options that do not interoperate well. When we are at work, we have a wireless PBX and a wireless LAN that use different infrastructures. When we are at home, we have a cordless phone. In the car, we have cellular service. In the plane, we have air phone. Can we get to the point where we can access all the networks we need with a single device without having to think about it as shown in Figure 1.5?

Can we use the same light, long battery life device to access the wireless PBX at the office as the system we have at home? Can we use that same device when we are in the car traveling in sparsely populated areas and access large cell systems by connecting to our higher power car-based system? Is it possible to have a base station in the plane that allows this same device to access air-to-ground circuits instead of using yet another distinct system for communicating from planes, and having to turn off our own systems for fear of interfering with the plane's navigation systems? Will we be able to carry these devices from one part of the country to another and have good coverage and seamless provision of the services we signed up for? Can we take our phones with us around the world? Will we have to subscribe to expensive satellite services to achieve worldwide roaming?

The Radio Spectrum

Most of the Wireless Networking services are crowded around 1 GHz as shown in Figure 1.6
Figure 1.6 shows the frequency ranges for extremely low frequencies, very low frequencies, medium frequencies, high frequencies, very high frequencies, ultra high frequencies, the microwave region, the infrared region, the visible light region, the ultra light region, and finally X rays. The audio frequencies that we hear range from 20 Hz to 20 KHz. AM radio stations are in the 100-KHz range. FM radio and TV are in the 100-MHz range. Paging systems fall in the 50- to 500-MHz range. Mobile radio and cellular systems use the band just below 1 GHz. Cordless and PCS systems use the bands around 2 GHz. The infrared region is huge. It has its applications in the Wireless LAN areas and in short range point-to-point communications including remote control systems.

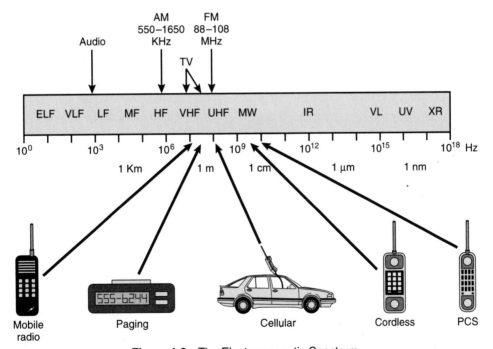

Figure 1.6   The Electromagnetic Spectrum.

Why are so many services crowded around 1 GHz, and why are future high density services moving to the 2-GHz bands? One reason is simply the availability of spectrum. The spectrum around 1 GHz is becoming full. To obtain greater bandwidth, we must move up in the frequency band. As we move up, the amount of bandwidth increases exponentially. The challenge is to build equipment that can operate at the higher frequencies and achieve acceptable range with reasonable power. Silicon as of a few years ago could only handle frequencies up to 1 GHz. Higher frequency systems were forced to use Gallium Arsenide that was more expensive at the time. Now Silicon can achieve greater speeds, and GaAs is becoming cost-effective.

The power and range challenges will remain; they are physical limits. More about those parameters in the next chapter.

Traffic Types and Technologies

Now, let us look at another kind of map of wireless technologies. This map is a matrix of technologies and traffic types. Figure 1.7 depicts the technologies vertically down the left side of the matrix, and the types of traffic along the horizontal axis. The number of stars indicates the degree of applicability of the technology to the traffic type. Four stars is the maximum. Cellular provides very good voice, but has only three stars. In order to conserve bandwidth, cellular systems use vocoding techniques such as Residually Excited Linear Predictive coding to reduce the rate of the voice signal down from 32 Kbps. Adaptive Delta Pulse Code Modulation (ADPCM), is used in the wired network to 13 Kbps or less.

For this reason, the quality of the voice, though quite good, is not as good as for the wired network. As coding techniques improve and processors become powerful and can implement more

	Voice	Data	Alert	Positioning
Cellular	* * *	* *		
Paging		* *	* * * *	
Packet radio		* * * *		
Satellite	* *	* *		* * *
Cordless	* * *	*		
PCS	* * * *	* *		

Figure 1.7   Traffic/technology matrix.

sophisticated algorithms effectively, the quality of the vocoded voice will rival that of the wired network.

Cellular can handle data on the order of 10 Kbps. Actually, at the present time, analog cellular with a cellular modem can handle up to 14.4 Kbps without compression, whereas digital cellular is limited to 9.6 Kbps. The reason for this is that analog cellular has leveraged the advances in modem technology for the wired network to extract an excellent data rate from an analog voice grade channel; whereas digital has a channel structure that is optimized for voice. Data are provided on voice equivalent channels, each of which can support a maximum of 9.6 Kbps. To achieve higher data rates, a number of voice channels have to be combined together. The initial standards do not provide for this capability. Proposals are being made to provide this combining in later phases of the standards.

The main aim of paging is to handle alert traffic. Alert traffic usually comprises a simple phone number that the calling party sends to the called party to alert them to return the call. It is one-way in its present form. The data rate is quite low, below 1 Kbps and it provides one-way service only. It is sometimes used for receiving short electronic mail, as well as for receiving other short messages. Advanced paging and two-way paging systems will rival packet radio networks in their ability to meet the demands of bursty traffic. Both two-way paging and packet radio networks are designed to carry bursty traffic effectively.

Satellite systems serve voice and data, but at greater expense and with much larger terminals at the present time. They are the prime technology for positioning systems. They have been used for this purpose for many years, particularly for maritime and aeronautical use. They are also used for other positioning applications that are land based and can provide great location accuracy.

Cordless telephony provides fairly good voice quality and little data. PCS is aimed at providing voice quality of equivalent quality as the wired network. The coding technique used for PCS systems is 32 Kbps ADPCM, same as for the wired network. The constraints on spectrum are not as tight for PCS systems as they are for cellular systems, because the cell sizes are smaller, and the spectrum can be reused more frequently. PCS can also provide greater data rates, since the data can use wider voice grade channels starting at 32 Kbps, and going up to the maximum data rate of the carrier. More about that in later chapters.

Cell Size and Achievable Throughput

Figure 1.8 is another very useful map of wireless services. This time the service types are plotted on a matrix of achievable data rate versus cell size.

The cell sizes vary from tens of meters to thousands of kilometers. There is a break in the horizontal axis between the tens of Km range and the thousands of Km range. In the upper left hand corner we have Wireless LANs. They provide data rates in the range of 1 Mbps. Their cell sizes are usually in the range of 50 m indoors. This figure is a nominal range that includes propagation through the walls inside a building.

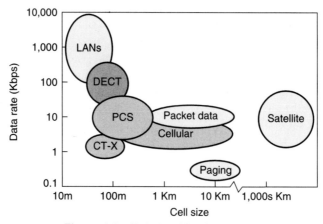

Figure 1.8 Relationship of networks.

On the other extreme are satellite services. The cell sizes can be thousands of Km and cover continents. The data rate that is usually provided is in the 10-Kbps range per channel. The total data rate for a whole transponder is much higher, but the typical data rate per channel is the 10-Kbps range.

On the lower extreme, are simple one-way paging systems. They provide very low data rates below 1 Kbps. The range of a paging base station can be quite large, tens of Km. This makes implementing a paging network relatively fast compared to a cellular network. For example, to install a paging network that covers most of the population of a small Asian country like Vietnam, a total investment on the order of $100 million and a time frame of about one year would be required.

The frequency allocation for a paging network is extremely small relative to the allocation required for a cellular, PCS, satellite, or Wireless LAN service. This bandwidth is used very efficiently to provide the service. Since the required bandwidth is so small, it is often allocated at a low frequency band that is much lower than the bands used by higher data rate services. The low frequency means that the cell sizes can be large while keeping the power relatively low. Advanced and two-way paging networks would move paging up and to the left towards packet data on the chart. This is because advanced and two-way paging networks provide higher data rates. The higher data rates require greater bandwidth. This size of allocation is not available at low frequency bands, so it is provided at higher frequencies. The higher frequencies require greater power to achieve the same range as the lower frequencies. In addition, the higher data rate in itself requires higher power to transmit.

Packet data networks have cells that can be tens of Km in size. Their data rates are on the order of 10 to 20 Kbps. This data rate is shared among the customers contending for the use of the channel. The sharing mechanism is usually a random access scheme typical of a Local Area Network. The total bandwidth allocated to a packet radio network is relatively small compared to the bandwidth allocated to a cellular service, a PCS service, a satellite service, or a LAN service. It is not as small as a one-way paging service, but it is not much more than the equivalent of one single voice channel in a cellular network. This bandwidth is then shared by all the data users who are typically sending transaction type traffic. The traffic is sent through the network on a store-and-forward basis. Depending on the application, extremely fast response time may not be needed. For example, for electronic mail, a response time of a few minutes may be acceptable. For an interactive session, a response time of less than one second would be required. Users of packet networks are charged on a flat monthly charge plus a charge per packet basis.

In the middle of the chart, we have cellular, cordless, and PCS services. The cell sizes for cellular can range from a few hundred meters, to tens of Km. The small cell sizes are for denser downtown areas, the larger are for more sparse densities. The data rates are on the order of 10 Kbps. Cordless systems have cell sizes around 100 meters. Many of them serve indoor or very dense urban areas. The data rates of CT-X systems that include CT-2 and CT-3 are on the same order as cellular. The definitions of CT-0 and CT-1 for cordless telephony in the home do not include digital data at this time. PCS promises to provide greater data throughput than cellular. DECT provides very high data rates for a service that is not LAN based. It provides on the order of 1/2 Mbps, coming close to what a Wireless LAN can provide.

The services are clustered along a curve that begins at the upper left-hand corner of the matrix and descends to the lower right-hand corner. There are no services in the upper right-hand corner, or the lower left-hand corner. In the upper right-hand corner, the data rate is high and the cell size is large. This is a very difficult situation to realize, because as the cell size increases, more and more people are likely to be in the cell. If each of them is demanding a large data rate, the service would have to provide a huge aggregate data rate.

At the lower-left hand corner, the data rate is low and the cell size is low. When the data rate is low, it is easy to make the cell size large, for example with paging, so we do not see many services in this corner. This does not mean that some niche services may not now exist, or some such services may not materialize in the future. One example would be an extremely low cost, very localized service that needs very little bandwidth.

Most of the services are grouped along a curve that implies that the higher the data rate, the smaller the cell size must be. The reasons are: The smaller the cell size, the more frequently the bandwidth can be reused, and the smaller the cell size, the less the power transmitted has to be.

In this book, we focus on the cellular area, the cordless and PCS area, and briefly on the satellite area to show how it fits in with cellular and PCS. First, we begin with some market forecasts for these areas.

Market Forecasts

The focus of this section is not on the exact magnitude of market sizes in different parts of the world for different services, but rather on the relative sizes. First, it is instructive to discuss the phases of growth of the cellular market, to follow this with a discussion of the development of the PCS market and then discuss the differences.

Analog Cellular

Figure 1.9 depicts the three stages of the growth of the cellular market. In stage 1, networks are rolled out to achieve 95 percent coverage. During this phase, terminal prices fall, and air time tariffs remain stable. We have seen this occur over the past few years. Initially, a cellular phone cost almost $3,000. Europe was the first to drop the handset price to zero if the customer signed up for the service for a period of time; North America followed suit about a year later. Meanwhile, the cost of the handset was still in excess of $1,000 in certain parts of Asia such as Hong Kong. Soon after, those prices began to drop as well. During this period, the air time tariffs remained stable. These low handset prices are subsidized by the network.

Next, as more and more service providers are allowed to enter the market, air time drop begins to drop as well. At the present time, we have two service providers of cellular services in most regions. It seems that two service providers are not sufficient to cause the price to drop dramatically; however, with three, four, and five service providers the competition will be significant. The resulting drop in price will stimulate the market, but may not necessarily be in the best interest of the industry in the long term due to the inefficiency of having that large a number of competitors. We will see later that spectrum utilization efficiency drops dramatically with this many competitors. Ultimately, the optimum number of service providers from the viewpoint of both efficiency and healthy competition may be three or four.

Digital Cellular

The second stage of the growth of cellular demand sees major market development. Digital takes the lead from analog and data services grow. This is stage 2 that lasts for about three years. The third and final stage lasts about seven years and sees declining analog services and market sharing of cellular with other services such as cordless and PCS. Before this time, all market segments grow sufficiently and there is little market interaction. But during stage 3, each kind of technology will claim the applications that best fit its unique capabilities. We are presently between stages 1 and 2.

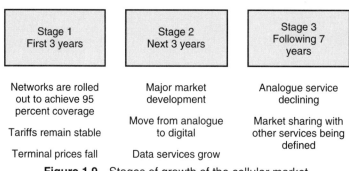

Figure 1.9   Stages of growth of the cellular market.

Figure 1.10 is interesting because it shows the interaction between analog cellular and digital cellular.

The implementation of analog cellular levels off in the middle of the chart. This leveling off takes place at different points in time in different parts of the world. As old analog systems go out of service, they are not replaced by new analog systems; they are replaced by digital systems. New demand is met by digital systems. Analog does not fall off quickly because there are many parts of the world that are served well by analog cellular, in particular, those areas with sparse population densities such as Scandinavian countries and certain parts of the United States. This is one reason why the digital cellular standard in the United States is dual mode. It is felt that such a dual mode standard is needed in order to allow the coexistence of both analog and digital cellular systems for some time in the future.

The typical life cycle of a product or service is depicted in Figure 1.11. This life cycle is very familiar. What is interesting is to apply it to the services under consideration here, namely, analog cellular, digital cellular, cordless, and PCS. As the shape in Figure 1.10 implies, analog cellular is in the maturation stage while digital cellular is definitely in the robust growth phase. It was in the early adopter phase for several years but now is in the robust growth phase in many parts of the world. Service providers are racing to put systems in place. Users are signing up for the service and are beginning to truly depend on it. Digital cellular will serve as the launching pad for future value-added systems.

Cordless Telephony

What about cordless and PCS systems? Cordless systems can be thought of in two different areas: residential cordless and cordless public telepoint systems. Residential cordless has been in the robust growth phase for some time in North America and in Japan. Its life cycle may wane as

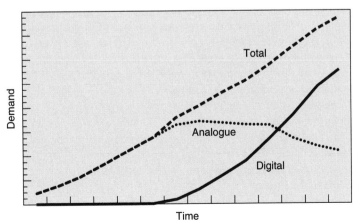

Figure 1.10 Long-term forecast for analog and digital cellular.

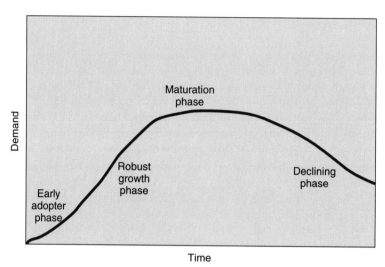

Figure 1.11   The life cycle of services.

high density low-tier PCS systems begin to be implemented in volume. Public cordless systems saw their early implementations in Europe and parts of Asia, but are already beginning to fall in popularity in favor of PCS systems. In fact, cordless systems can be considered in some ways to be the early adopter phase of PCS.

High-tier PCS

To discuss PCS fully, we need to consider both high-tier PCS and low-tier PCS. These types of PCS are discussed in detail in later chapters. The high-tier PCS systems are small-cell cellular systems. The low-tier systems are extremely small cell, very high density, and probably lower cost systems. Examples of high-tier PCS are DCS systems; examples of low-tier PCS systems are PACS or DECT. High-tier PCS will come first, grow and mature, while low-tier, very high density PCS systems with many more cell sites will follow.

These ideas are depicted in Figure 1.12.

Analog cellular peaks and begins to mature as digital cellular rapidly grows. Meanwhile, public access cordless systems such as CT-2 telepoint systems are in the declining phase. To replace them we have high-tier PCS systems that are just beginning to be implemented in North America, Europe, parts of Asia, and other parts of the world as well. Low-tier, very high density will follow some time in the future.

Figure 1.13 shows the situation and reflects the point in time where the different services are at the present.

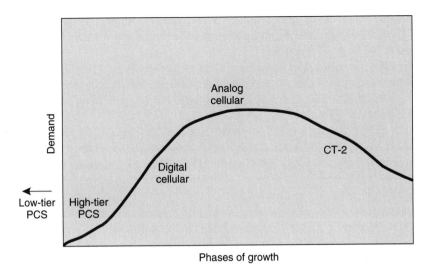

Figure 1.12   The phases of growth of cellular and related services.

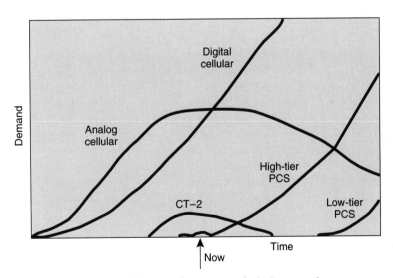

Figure 1.13   The growth patterns of wireless services.

Digital cellular is picking up the bulk of the demand of cellular from the maturing analog cellular. CT-2 has essentially come and gone as it becomes replaced by high-tier PCS systems. Later, low-tier PCS comes on stream.

Will high-tier and low-tier PCS systems be implemented at the expense of digital cellular? This is an important question that is causing some confusion in the industry. The answer in the long term is: not much. The two services have significantly different design points and meet different market demands that are complementary.

Will high-tier PCS replace the demand for cellular? The answer to this question is not as clear. The design points for cellular and high-tier PCS are closer together. High-tier PCS is best suited for dense urban areas, whereas cellular is best suited for the areas between the high density centers. In the third phase of the development of the cellular market, the market shares among these services will be defined by the market.

Next, let us consider the relative sizes of the PCS market in different regions of the world. Frequently, market forecasts for the world are divided in the following regions:

- North America
- Europe
- Pacific Rim
- Rest of the world.

Figure 1.14 shows the relative sizes of the markets in these parts of the world for PCS. The vertical axis is the percent market share for each region of the world. Even though each part of the world is experiencing accelerating growth, some parts are starting later than others; and furthermore, in

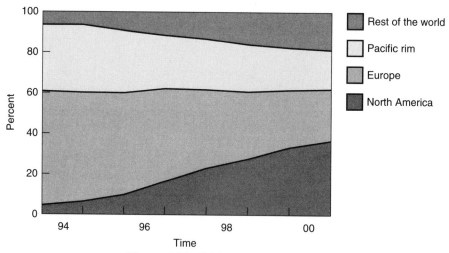

Figure 1.14   PCS market by region.

some cases are overtaking the areas that had early starts. In particular, North America starts out last but ends up in the lead on a relative basis. Whether the market develops as predicted will depend on many factors including the degree of competition allowed in different parts of the world, and thereby affecting price and resulting market size. It may very well be that the four regions of the world will garner about equal market shares rather than North America commanding a greater portion as shown above. This may take place because of greater than anticipated growth in the Pacific Rim and other parts of the world.

Finally, let us examine the relative functionality and cost of digital cellular, analog cellular, high-tier PCS, and low-tier PCS. Figure 1.15 shows the mobility a user can achieve with each service and the relative cost of providing each service.

Low-tier PCS

The goal of low-tier PCS is definitely to be a low-cost local service with islands of very small cell sizes and very low power. The cost is very low per user. The challenge is to have a very large number of users to amortize the large number of cell sites. Each cell site may be quite a bit less expensive than the cell site of a higher tier service, but there are so many more cell sites that it becomes a daunting task to implement such a service initially when the demand is not mature. That is why its implementation is likely to come at a later time.

The same argument applies for the difference in implementation costs of high-tier PCS and cellular. High-tier PCS systems will also have many more cell sites than cellular, but they are intended to serve many more users, so the cost per user served can be lower.

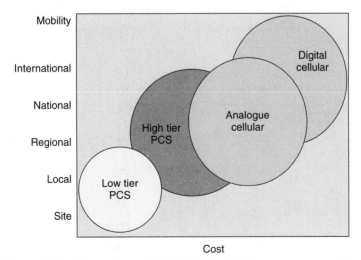

Figure 1.15 Comparison of GSM, DCS, DECT, and analog cellular.

Summary

In this chapter we have discussed the cellular, cordless, and PCS markets. We discussed market forecasts for four major areas of the world: North America, Europe, the Pacific Rim, and the rest of the world. North America starts out last but garners roughly an equal if not slightly larger share compared with the other regions of the world. We discussed the three phases of growth of the cellular market. We showed the relative mobility and cost of digital cellular, analog cellular, high-tier PCS, and low-tier PCS.

We put these services into perspective by presenting several wireless maps. The first map showed the evolution of products and services as well as the standards and spectra for wireless networking activities throughout the world including not just cellular and PCS but also Wireless LANs and Mobile Data services. We presented a map of data rate and cell size that compared the services and analyzed their present relationship. We discussed the applications of different kinds of user traffic to each kind of service. Next, we will discuss propagation formulas and modulation techniques.

2 Radio Propagation and Modulation Techniques

Wireless services are mostly carried in the microwave radio band. Designing an efficient and reliable system in this band hinges upon a good understanding of how signals propagate in this medium, the impairments of the signals due to fading and multipath, and ways of dealing with them. The available frequency spectrum is shared among its users through frequency, time, and code division multiple access. How do these techniques compare? Which is the most effective for which service? What is the performance of each technique? In this chapter, we discuss:

- Radio propagation principles
  - Propagation results
  - Rayleigh fading
  - Multipath and intersymbol interference
- Modulation techniques
  - Frequency shift keying
  - Phase shift keying
  - Gaussian shift keying
  - Others
- Signal coding
  - Error detection and correction
  - Voice coding including CELP and VSELP
- Duplexing methods
  - Frequency Division Duplexing
  - Time Division Duplexing
- Multiple access alternatives and comparisons
  - Frequency Division Multiple Access

Layer 3	**Network**	**Internet protocols**
Layer 2	Data Link	Logical Link Control (LLC)
		Medium Access Control (MAC)
Layer 1	Physical	Physical (PHY)

Figure 2.1   Protocol layers.

- Time Division Multiple Access
- Code Division Multiple Access
- CDMA examples
- The TDMA/ CDMA debate
- Cellularization techniques

Most Wireless Networks are an implementation of the first two layers of Open Systems Interconnection (OSI) protocol stack. Figure 2.1 shows the first three layers of the OSI protocol stack. The first layer is the physical or PHY layer. The second layer is the data link layer and has two sublayers, the Medium Access Control sublayer, and the Logical Link Control sublayer. The third layer is the network layer.

The responsibility of the physical layer is to transmit bits over the medium. Once a modulation technique is chosen, the channel capacity is determined, so that given an allocation of so many MHz, we can determine how many Mbps we can achieve. A typical number is 1 bps per Hz. To get more than 1 bps per Hz, we have to use higher order modulation as we will discuss shortly. Almost all transmission is modulated onto a carrier of some frequency—the carrier frequency in the center of the allocated bandwidth. In rare occasions, the information is sent at baseband. The most notable example is infrared transmission where the IR energy is turned on and off rapidly to correspond directly to the ones and zeros in the bit stream. All of the cellular, cordless, and PCS systems use a modulated scheme.

The responsibility of the MAC sublayer is to allow sharing of the channels of the medium. The LLC is where the framing is performed. A frame typically includes a header with information such as the source address, the destination address and other control information, and the data bits, followed by some sort of error detection and perhaps error correction bits. This is illustrated in Figure 2.2 where SA is the Source Address, DA is the Destination Address, and EDC is Error Detection and Correction.

Figure 2.2   Frame format and LLC functions.

The network layer is where routing among different networks is carried out. The higher four layers are the transport layer where handling of acknowledgments (ACKs and NACKs) and flow control are performed. Above the network layer there is the session layer, the presentation layer, and the application layer.

Most Wireless Networking products are PHY and MAC implementations. We sometimes have to be involved with the networking layer, for example, when we have to deal with a large system with multiple distinct networks. For these cases, we will discuss modifications to the Internet Protocol to allow it to handle mobile devices. This is now defined as Mobile IP.

Radio Propagation

In this section, we develop basic propagation formulas starting out with intuitive ideas. The propagation formulas show the fundamental trade-offs in cellular systems. They show why higher frequency systems such as DCS 1800 are aimed at smaller cell applications while lower frequency GSM 900 systems are aimed at larger cell applications covering larger urban areas. They also show why it is sometimes necessary to go near a window when making a cellular call inside a building even with the power levels of GSM.

Figure 2.3 shows the basic parameters. The base station transmits P_t watts from an antenna with gain G_t. A distance d away, a receiver receives P_r from an antenna with gain G_r. The received power is given in terms of the transmitted power, the distance, the antenna gains, the speed of light, and the frequency by the following formula:

$$P_r = (P_t/4\pi d^2) G_t G_r (c^2/4\pi f^2) \tag{2.1}$$

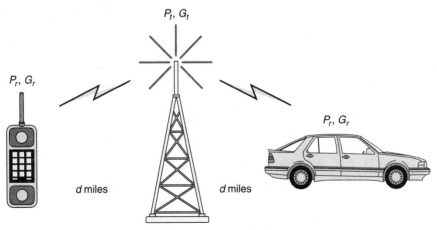

Figure 2.3   Radio propagation parameters.

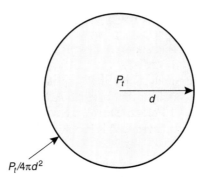

Figure 2.4   The spreading of the transmitted power.

Intuitively, the first term is the power transmitted by the base station spread out over a sphere with surface area $4\pi d^2$ as shown in Figure 2.4. So, the power falls as the square of the distance. The next term in eq. (2.1) is $G_t\,G_r$, the antenna gain of the transmitter and the antenna gain of the receiver. The more the gains, the more power is received. The antenna gains in effect focus the energy into specific areas, so it does not spread out into unneeded directions.

A typical antenna pattern has a kind of donut shape without a hole as shown in Figure 2.5. This antenna pattern is generated by a simple antenna that is a half or a quarter wavelength long. This antenna pattern works quite well in most cellular applications, since we are mostly interested in transmitting in the horizontal direction. We are not concerned with covering the volume directly above the cell site, since cellular is not intended to cover flying objects. Also we are not concerned with coverage directly below the cell site. When the user is that close to the cell site, there is plenty of transmitted energy anyway.

The last term in eq. (2.1) is $(c^2/4\pi f^2)$ and shows that the power received decreases as the square of the frequency. This is an important idea, since it makes a large difference as we move higher and higher in frequency. As time goes on and the demand for cellular and PCS systems ma-

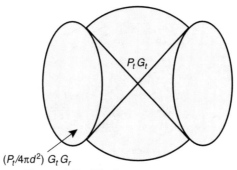

Figure 2.5   Dipole antenna pattern.

tures, we will need more and more bandwidth. One way to obtain that bandwidth is to move higher and higher in the frequency spectrum. As we do, the range of the systems will be limited for the same transmitted power and antenna gains. In fact, DCS 1800 achieves only one quarter of the range as GSM 900 for the same transmitted power. Put another way, to achieve the same range, DCS 1800 would require four times the power as GSM 900.

One would expect that for this reason DCS 1800 systems would then be built with higher power than GSM 900, but the inverse is true. DCS power levels are 1 watt and below, GSM 900 power levels are usually 2 watts, and can go up to 8, and even to 20 watts. The result is that DCS 1800 systems have much smaller cell sizes than GSM 900 systems and apply to denser applications. Trying to cover large sparsely populated areas such as roads with DCS 1800 would require a great many base stations and may not be economical. That is the job for a low frequency, large cell technology such as GSM 900.

We can rewrite eq. (2.1) in terms of the free space loss L_o as follows:

$$P_r = P_t G_t G_r / L_o \tag{2.2}$$

where

$$\text{Free space loss} = L_o = (4\pi df/c)^2. \tag{2.3}$$

Radio engineers work in dBs. A dB is $10 \log_{10}$ of the quantity. A factor of 10 is 10 dB. A factor of 100 is 20 dB. A factor of a million is 60 dB. Expressing eq. (2.3) in dBs yields:

$$L_o \text{ dB} = 32 + 20 \log f \text{ MHz} + 20 \log d \text{ Km}. \tag{2.4}$$

Now the frequency is expressed in MHz and the distance is expressed in Km to make it easier to substitute in typical values. For example, typical values for a cellular system are $f = 1$ GHz, and $d = 1$ Km. For these values, $L_o = 92$ dB. This means that the free space loss is more than a factor of 10^{-9}. In other words, one billionth of the power transmitted arrives at the receiver.

Antenna gains for half-wave dipoles that have the antenna pattern shown in Figure 2.5 are about 1.8 dB, not very much. The wavelength at 1 GHz is 30 cm, so half the wavelength is 15 cm, and a quarter is 7.5 cm. Those are the antennas that we find in most cellular hand-sets. The antenna gains of a parabolic antenna such as those used with satellites is given in terms of its physical size A by:

$$G = (4\pi c^2/f^2) A. \tag{2.5}$$

The larger the physical size of the parabola, the greater the gain. For Geostationary satellites, such an antenna is required. A satellite phone fills a heavy briefcase and costs more than \$10,000. For deep space astronomical exploration, extremely large antennas are used. There is a huge antenna in South America that is built by running cables in a valley between mountains, and the collector is hanging between the mountain tops!

Ultimately, to receive the signal successfully, we must achieve a required signal to noise ratio at the receiver. Therefore, we need to express the above equations in terms of a required signal to noise ratio.

$$\text{Required } (S/N) = P_r / N_r = P_t G_t G_r / L_o N_r. \tag{2.6}$$

Rearranging terms, we find that the transmitted power must be:

$$P_t \text{ dB} > \text{required } (S/N) + N_r + L_o - G_t - G_r. \tag{2.7}$$

The transmitted power must provide the needed signal-to-noise ratio, overcome the ambient noise and the free space loss, and at the same time be aided by the antenna gains.

Typical receivers require signal to noise ratios in the range of 18 dB, and typical ambient noise densities are −120 dBm (dBm is a dB relative to a milliwatt). Continuing our example with half dipole antennas having gains of about 1.5 dB, and the free space loss of 92 dB, we find that:

$$P_t \text{ dB} > -13 \text{ dBm} = 0.05 \text{ mw.} \tag{2.8}$$

The transmitted power needs to be only 5/100th of a milliwatt. That is a tiny amount compared to the values we find in real life of 2 watts and 0.6 watts. Well, so far we have accounted only for free space loss.

The deviations from free space loss in real life include loss due to building clutter as well as clutter resulting from other obstacles, and the loss when the user is inside a building, and the base station is outside the building. This is the case for most large and medium cell size cellular systems—the real loss is given by:

$$L = \text{Free space loss} + \text{building clutter} + \text{for inside buildings,}$$
$$L = L_o + (20 \text{ to } 30) \text{ dB} + (20 \text{ to } 30) \text{ dB.} \tag{2.9}$$

Carrying on the example, we now have to increase the 0.05 mw by a factor of 100 to 1,000 to account for building clutter. That increases it to 5 to 50 mw. And we have to increase it by another factor of 100 to 1,000 in order to be able to operate inside buildings. That raises it to 0.5 to 5 w. As it happens, cellular systems use 0.6 w to 2 w, and sometimes we have to go near the window in order to get acceptable reception. This example shows why that occurs.

What can we do to improve the situation for working inside buildings? The ultimate answer involves smaller cells, and eventually cell sites inside the building with high density systems such as PCS.

Fading Channels

Now, let us take a closer look at the impairments that buildings and other obstacles cause. Figure 2.6 shows a typical scenario in a downtown area. In most cases, the cell site is not even within line of site of the user, so the only signals reaching him or her are refracted and reflected signals. Some of the reflected objects may be moving such as passing airplanes. The situation is even more difficult for a pedestrian than for a vehicle, because pedestrians are more easily shaded by obstacles.

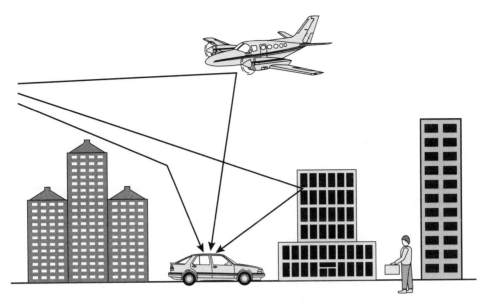

Figure 2.6 Multipath.

The multiple signals interfere at the receiver and can cause fading. The signals arrive out of phase and in effect cancel each other. This kind of fading occurs if the signals arrive one-half of a wavelength apart, and is called fast fading. We have all experienced this kind of fading when listening to an FM station in the car. FM radio frequencies are in the range of 100 MHz, so the wavelength is about 3 meters. As we come to a stoplight while listening to an FM station that has been coming in weakly, it is possible to stop at such a point where the station fades out completely. By moving the car slightly, we once more regain good reception. The movement is on the order of one meter, and that changes the multipath situation sufficiently to eliminate the severe cancellation. The wavelength at 1 GHz is 30 cm so even smaller movements can change the effect of fast fading. Slow fading is due to large movements. These movements cause general reduction of the received energy, as, for example, when the receiver moves behind a large obstruction that is between it and the base station transmitter.

As we can see in Figure 2.6, real life situations defy description by the simple formulas we just developed. How are we to design systems in such environments where any number of reflections can arrive at the receiver, and the situation continuously changes? Fortunately, there is a model called the Rayleigh model that is very simple to calculate, but agrees with real life surprisingly well. In the Rayleigh model, we assume that:

- The fading is flat within the frequency band of interest, so the fading is not selective within the band of our signal
- There are many reflections arriving at the receiver

- They are of roughly equal amplitude
- Their phase is uniformly distributed between 0 and 360 degrees.

These assumptions may not seem reasonable in all cases, but let's see how the model performs. First, the closed form description of the received power is given by:

$$\text{Probability } (P_r < x) = 1 - \exp\left(-x^2 / 2\sigma^2\right), \tag{2.10}$$

where σ^2 is the mean power received. This is a very simple formulation that is easily graphed as shown in Figure 2.7. The solid line is the formulation; the squares are measured data from real life experiments. As can be seen, the theory agrees extremely well with real life.

We cannot state the received power deterministically, but we can express the probability that the received power is less than some value. This is quite good enough in practice, since we can then state that 99 percent of the time, the received power is above a certain value, and therefore the error probability is below what is required.

In addition to causing fading, both fast and slow, multipath can also cause intersymbol interference. This does not happen in all situations; in some cases, multipath can actually help by getting back some of the energy. This is illustrated in Figure 2.8.

As we can see, in the first case, the reflected signals arrive within a fraction of the bit length, and the sum of the signals is actually larger than the first signal alone. In this case, multipath enhances the received signal. This is a common occurrence, and is often counted on and used as part of the design of systems. Such a system is called Rake filtering.

In the second case, the reflections arrive a significant portion of the bit length later and cause interference. The reflection of the first bit arrives on top of a significant part of the second bit and causes Inter Symbol Interference (ISI).

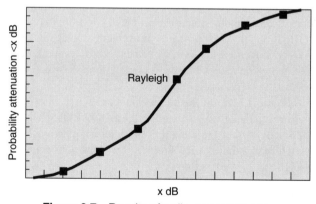

Figure 2.7   Results of radio measurements.

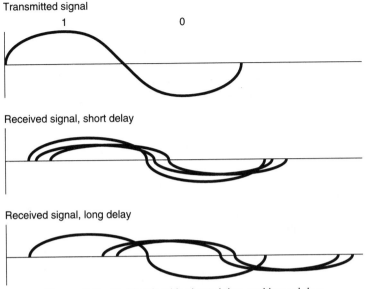

Transmitted signal

Received signal, short delay

Received signal, long delay

Figure 2.8 Multipath with short delay and long delay.

Can this latter destructive situation arise in real life situations? Absolutely—Delay times often match or exceed the bit lengths of the signal. A path length difference of 1 Km, causes delay of:

$$\text{delay} = \text{distance difference} / c = 1,000 / (3 \times 10^8) = 3.33 \ \mu s. \tag{2.11}$$

If the signal data rate is 100 Kbps, the bit length is 10 μs, and the reflections arrive 1/3 of the bit later, and does cause ISI. We can either withstand the ISI, and the resulting increased error rate, or take some proactive measures to counteract the ISI.

For most cellular systems, we do take proactive measures to deal with ISI. The two choices are equalization and rake filtering. Equalization looks for the reflected signal in the composite received signal and cancels it out. Rake filtering is more intelligent. It looks for the reflected signal and constructively adds it back in. Both these methods are commonly used in cellular systems.

For indoor systems, the same phenomena occur, but the order of magnitude is different. The reflections come from walls in the building, not from whole buildings, or mountains, so the distance differences are much smaller. They are typically on the order of 100 m. A path length difference of 100 m would cause a delay of 0.33 μs. This delay becomes a problem when the data rate of the signal is above 1 Mbps where the bit length is 1 μs. Therefore, we can transmit much higher date rates indoors before multipath starts to become a problem.

Modulation Techniques

In this section, we discuss how to modulate the information onto the carrier frequency. The three major modulation techniques are illustrated in Figure 2.9.

An example of each kind of modulation is shown. In the first case, AM, the information is in the amplitude of the signal. The signal can be written as follows:

$$s(t) = m(t) \cos \omega t. \tag{2.12}$$

For FM, the information is in the frequency of the carrier. The signal can be written as:

$$s(t) = m(t) \cos [\omega + bm(t)] t, \tag{2.13}$$

where, b is the modulation index. We can increase the fidelity of the signal by increasing the modulation index, b. This requires more bandwidth. Thus, we can trade bandwidth for fidelity. For PM, the information is in the phase of the carrier.

The most common digital modulation techniques are forms of Frequency Shift Keying and Phase Shift Keying. These two modulation techniques are illustrated in Figure 2.10.

For FSK, the frequency is shifted between two frequencies, one just above the center frequency, and the other just below it. This is the simplest form of FSK, it is binary FSK with no shaping. For PSK, the phase of the signal is shifted by 180 degrees. This is equivalent to sending the negative of the signal and is the simplest form of PSK. It is binary PSK with no shaping.

Binary PSK is formed as shown in Figure 2.11. The binary bit stream is first put through a binary comparator. This converts the [0,1] bit stream into a [−1,+1] stream. The binary comparator allows us to minimize the DC component of the signal and therefore be able to use low pass filtering at the receiver to reduce noise. Next, the signal is multiplied by the local oscillator running at the carrier frequency to yield the Radio Frequency signal.

When we obtain a spectrum allocation from the regulatory agency, they specify the power limits and the amount of energy within the specified bandwidth, as well as outside that bandwidth. They specify a spectrum mask within which we have to stay so as not to interfere with other users in adjacent bands. It is physically impossible to create signals that have no energy whatsoever outside a specified band, but we can create signals that can have very small components outside a specified band. We do this by using a channel filter as shown in Figure 2.11.

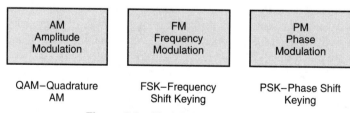

Figure 2.9   Modulation techniques.

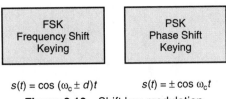

$$s(t) = \cos(\omega_c \pm d)t \qquad s(t) = \pm \cos \omega_c t$$

Figure 2.10 Shift key modulation.

The channel filter has an impulse response given by $f(t)$. There are many channel filters possible. Radio engineers can discuss such filters and other variations on the modulation scheme for hours, such as at standards meetings where these discussions go on for months! The discussions are very interesting, but the difference in performance is not that great.

A very common channel filter has a Gaussian shape. The $f(t)$ is described in the frequency domain by:

$$F(\omega) = \exp -0.54 \, (\omega/\omega_c). \tag{2.14}$$

This function has the familiar Gaussian shape shown in Figure 2.12. The width of the pulse shape can be adjusted by the parameter in the formula. For example, we sometimes see 0.39 GMSK. This means that 39 percent of the energy is within the 3 dB points of the pulse shape.

One last point to discuss before going on to signal coding is Shanon's Theorem. This comes into play when discussing the merits of CDMA versus TDMA. The Theorem is also interesting in providing insight as to how well we are doing in modem technology, and how much further we have to go to achieve the maximum throughput that is theoretically possible. The Theorem states

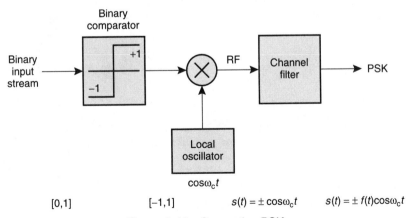

Figure 2.11 Gonerating PSK.

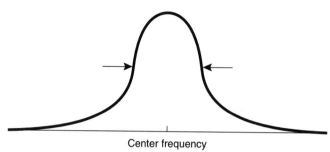

Center frequency

Figure 2.12   Gaussian pulse shape.

that the maximum data rate of a channel is given in terms of the bandwidth and the signal to noise ratio on the channel by:

$$R_{max} = B \log_2 (1 + S/N). \tag{2.15}$$

The Theorem states that in order to approach this limit, the modulated waveform needs to approach white noise. This is the argument put forth by the proponents of CDMA. They state that the information in essence modulates a noiselike carrier, namely the pseudo random code. Therefore, CDMA has the potential of achieving the maximum theoretical throughput of the channel and thus can use the precious spectrum most efficiently.

It is of interest to work out an example of Shanon's Theorem for a case we are very familiar with, the analog telephone channel. These connections can vary a bit, but on the average, the bandwidth is about 3 KHz, and the signal to noise ratio is about 20 dB, or a factor of 100. Substituting these values in eq. (2.14) yields a maximum data rate of about 20 Kbps. Today we have analog modems that exceed this. They can burst to 28.8 Kbps and with compression achieve 56.6 Kbps. Do they violate Shanon's Theorem? No—The bandwidth, or signal to noise of the channel does vary depending on the specific connection, and when it does these modems capitalize on the improvement and increase the data rate. In any case, they are doing extremely well. They have come a long way from 1200 bps of years past.

Signal Coding

There are four kinds of signal coding that can take place on the signal before transmission:

- Voice coding
- Data compression
- Error detection and correction coding
- Security coding.

Voice Coding

Voice coding technology has progressed to the point where we can have acceptable voice quality with 8 Kbps coding rates. The standards are all set to accept the next step in coding improvement; these are the half-rate codecs that promise to double the capacity of cellular systems when they become available. Voice coding depends on two major factors to be successful. First, is the pure mathematics. Second, is the processors to implement the mathematics in small, lightweight, battery-powered phones. The mathematics has been developed over a number of years, and most of the work is done. The challenge today is to have processors that are powerful enough, and use batteries efficiently enough to be practical in small phones. The progress of processors is continuing every year, so it is just a question of time before we can have the lower bit rate codecs in place. Examples of coding techniques are Residually Excited Linear Predictive coding. The coding uses the smooth nature of most voice waveforms to predict what the rest of the waveform will look like. It relies on the fact that the different parts of the waveform are highly correlated with other parts. It is possible that we may see coding rates as low as 2 Kbps or even 1 Kbps.

Data Compression

Data compression also aims at reducing the redundancy in the information. There are compression standards that are used in modems today that are double the effective data rate mentioned above.

Error Detection and Correction Coding

Error detection and correction coding take many forms. In its simplest form it inserts a few bits at the end of the frame to allow for the detection of errors in the information. One example utilized in error detection is Circular Redundancy Check. In its more complex forms, it inserts many more bits and actually is able to correct some errors. Typically, error correcting codes can correct on the order of 25 percent of the errors. They work best when the errors do not occur in sequence. However, in most real cases errors do occur in sequence when an impairment occurs on the channel. To counteract this, the information data are often interleaved, or put out of order in a specific way. This interleaving is reversed at the receiver. In this way, when an impairment on the channel does destroy several bits, they are actually not in sequence, and the error correcting code can perform well.

Error correcting codes can require many extra bits that do not carry information. However, this can be overdone. How much we do depends on the trade-off between always sending the overhead bits versus accepting errors and retransmitting the data. When the channel is expensive, more error correction is warranted; when the channel is cheap, less is in order. For example, cellular uses more error correction than cordless. Space communications systems especially deep space systems such as those exploring other planets, Mars for instance, use an extreme amount of error correction. PCS systems do not typically use error correction—they rely only on error detection.

Security Coding

Security coding encrypts the data according to some secret key. Digital cellular and PCS systems offer this as an option. If all the coding steps take place, we have the transmitter block diagram shown in Figure 2.13.

The first step, source coding, refers to either voice coding, such as RELP, or data compression. Next, we have encryption for security coding, followed by EDC coding, multiplexing, and transmission coding, which is the channel filter discussed previously that shapes the waveform to fit inside the mask specified by the regulatory agency. The modulation, the multiple access, and finally the RF transmitter are next. The receiver is the inverse of the above and is shown in Figure 2.14. Not all these steps are always present, so the diagram depicts a rather complex example to illustrate all the steps that could be present.

To put the ideas of source coding discussed in this section together, consider the following example:

- We start with an analog voice call
- We encode it using an 8 Kbps vocoder
- Next, we add signaling, which increases the rate to 9.6 Kbps
- With error detection and correction, we reach 19.2 Kbps
- This base-band signal then modulates a carrier using some form of FSK, or PSK.

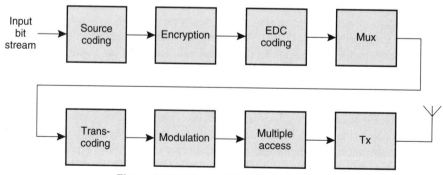

Figure 2.13 Transmitter block diagram.

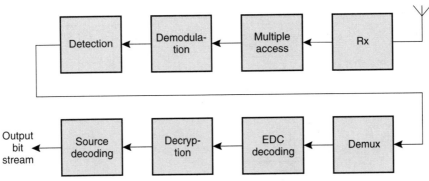

Figure 2.14 Receiver block diagram.

Multiplexing Techniques

Now that we have discussed modulation techniques, we know how many bps we will obtain from the MHz we have been allocated. Next, we have to decide how to divide this bandwidth into channels and then how to assign these channels to the users of the system. There are four options for this division or multiplexing:

- Frequency Division Multiplexing
- Time Division Multiplexing
- Code Division Multiplexing
- Combinations of the above.

The three basic techniques are illustrated in Figure 2.15.

FDM, TDM, and CDM

For FDM, each channel is a slice of frequency. That slice lasts as long as the call lasts. FDM is the oldest form of multiplexing and simple to implement. In TDM, each channel has a time slice for each frame; therefore, the time slice shown in the figure is repeated every frame for the duration of the call. Still, each channel occupies a different part of the frequency/time space. For CDM, this is no longer true. Each channel uses the whole frequency band and the same time for the duration of each call. The different channels are coincident on the same frequency/time space. They are distinguished by the pseudo random code they modulate.

Carrying on with the above example, we start with the 19.2 Kbps signal that includes error detection and correction. We now modulate a pseudo random code that is running at 1.23 Mcps

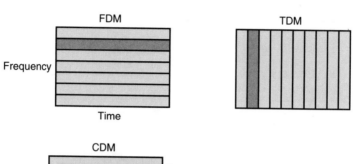

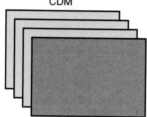

Figure 2.15   Multiplexing techniques.

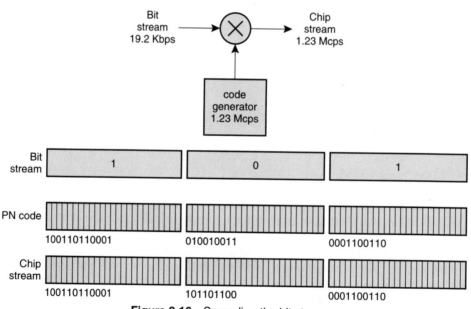

Figure 2.16   Spreading the bit stream.

and transmit this wide band signal on the air at the same time and in the same frequency spectrum as the other signals. How we combine the bit stream and the chip stream is an art of deriving the maximum orthogonality among the code division channels. To illustrate this principle, let us consider the very simple example shown in Figure 2.16.

The information bit stream is a 1 0 1. The pseudo random code is a long stream of chips. Also, the code does not repeat for many chips (on the order of 30,000 for practical systems). The longer the code, the more channels we can derive from it. The longer the code, the more complex are the circuits needed to decode it. The more complex the circuits, the more expensive they are, and more battery power is needed to operate them. The coding illustrated in the figure simply sends the code itself if the information bit is a 1, and sends the inverse of the code if the information bit is a 0. By the way, the word chip does not stand for anything, just like the word bit. A chip is called a different name than a bit to distinguish it from a bit, and to signify that there are many more chips than there are bits.

The result of the spreading is that the signal that goes out on the air is very wide bandwidth, with very low power spectral density. In fact, its spectral energy may be so low that it is below the ambient noise and is not visible to outside observers. This property of the signal made it attractive in defense applications, and that is where this technology was born.

Duplexing Techniques

Most cellular and PCS systems provide full duplex channels. A full duplex channel is essentially two separate channels, one for each direction of transmission. The alternative is simplex, which is commonly used in earlier mobile radio systems or walkie-talkie systems. Having two channels, one for each direction of transmission, allows a more natural conversation. In a normal conversation, one person speaks, the other person listens, and then interrupts briefly and begins to speak. While one person is speaking, there are pauses in his or her speech while the person takes a breath, or thinks of what to say. This is illustrated in Figure 2.17.

The total occupancy of the two channels is usually fairly low, on the order of 30 percent. This is not always so, for example, if one person is speaking most of the time, the ratio would be much higher. Such conversations often take place! So why have such an inefficient operation? It is to provide that natural transition from one speaker to the other. Without it, we would have a simplex channel and each person would have to capture the channel to speak. While one person is speaking, the other would not be able to interrupt and start speaking.

There is often confusion as to whether Local Area Networks are simplex or full duplex. Local Area Networks serve a wholly different kind of traffic. They serve transaction-based traffic, or single datagrams. A user typically listens to the channel, and there is one large bandwidth channel that is shared among all the users. If no one is transmitting, the user sends his packet and then stops. The packet is destined to one other or to several other users. A channel is not set up for con-

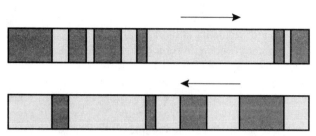

Figure 2.17   Typical loading of a full duplex channel.

tinuing communications between two users as is the common case in cellular and PCS systems. This is a connection-based system. Local Area Networks are connectionless based.

To provide full duplex channels, there are two methods, Frequency Division Duplexing and Time Division Duplexing. FDD is most commonly used in cellular systems, TDD is most commonly used in PCS systems that have smaller cell sizes. The reason for this is that TDD requires tighter synchronization and is easier to achieve in small cell PCS systems than in larger cell cellular systems.

Frequency Division Duplexing

FDD is illustrated in Figure 2.18. The pair of channels are separated in frequency. The pair is allocated to the cellular call for its duration. The lower channel is used by the mobile-to-base direction to make it as easy as possible for the battery powered mobile. The higher channel is used by the base station to mobile direction. In the cellular systems that we will discuss in the next chapter

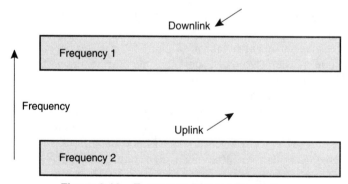

Figure 2.18   Frequency Division Duplexing.

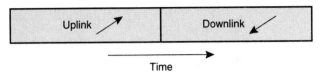

Figure 2.19   Time Division Duplexing.

we will see that the pairs of channels are separated by a significant distance in frequency. This is done in order to make the radio design easier. The more the separation, the simpler the filters are between transmitting and receiving filters.

Time Division Duplexing

Time Division Duplexing is illustrated in Figure 2.19. In this case, each direction of the conversation uses a separate time slot. This technique is sometimes called "Ping Pong." Tighter synchronization is required to make this method work effectively. Tight controls are not easy to achieve when cell sizes are large, and in addition, the variation in arrival times of the signals for a mobile that is close to the base station and one that is far from the base station is also large.

Media Access Control Techniques

Now that we have the channels defined, we need to discuss how to grant access to these channels to the users sharing the medium. This is the domain of the MAC sublayer, so now we move up to that level in Figure 2.20, which is reproduced here for convenience. The responsibility of the MAC layer is to define the protocol for users to obtain access to channels. Right above the

Layer 3	Network	Internet protocols
Layer 2	Data link	Logical Link Control (LLC)
		Medium Access Control (MAC)
Layer 1	Physical	Physical (PHY)

Figure 2.20   Protocol layers.

MAC is the LLC, where framing, addressing and error control are performed. The major MAC alternatives are:

- Frequency Division Multiple Access
- Time Division Multiple Access
- Code Division Multiple Access
- Carrier Sense Multiple Access
- Combinations and variations.

The most common protocols for cellular systems are FDMA and TDMA and combined FDMA/TDMA. CDMA is a recent addition that is receiving a lot of attention on a global basis. CSMA is primarily a Local Area Network protocol. It does appear in cellular networks in a subtle way. There is usually a random access part to the frame in most cellular networks to allow users to request a channel. The protocol in these parts is a form of random access scheme similar to CSMA.

FDMA, TDMA, and CDMA are deterministic protocols. When a user needs a channel, he requests a channel from a control point. The control point grants a channel that is available to that user for the duration of the call. The bandwidth is guaranteed for the duration of the call. This is the kind of scheme that is best for voice, video, and other traffic types that require guaranteed bandwidth. This kind of traffic is called isochronous traffic. There have been experiments of putting isochronous traffic over random access networks such as LANs, but the results have not been encouraging. The packet delays have a large variance causing them to get out of order resulting in unacceptable performance. ATM technology has changed that situation, since it can provide both guaranteed bandwidth with very low variance in packet delivery times, as well as extremely fast access time to the channel to satisfy asynchronous traffic.

Frequency Division Multiple Access

To illustrate each of the above, we can look first at AMPS that uses FDMA. The allocation for AMPS in the United States is:

- Portable transmits at 824 to 849 MHz = 25 MHz
- Base transmits at 869 to 894 MHz = 25 MHz.

To provide full duplexing, two frequency bands are allocated. The lower band is usually allocated for the transmission from the portable to the base station. This is done in order to make it as easy as possible for the portable. The higher band is for the base station to transmit. Each band is 25-MHz wide. These two bands are divided into pairs of channels each of which is 30-KHz wide. Each pair of channels is needed for one voice call in FDMA.

Time Division Multiple Access

Digital TDMA is actually combined FDMA/TDMA. Each 30-KHz channel is broken down into 3 TDMA channels, thus tripling the capacity of FDMA AMPS. In this case, each channel is a pair of frequency/time slices that repeat every frame until the call in completed. This is illustrated in Figure 2.21.

Code Division Multiple Access

In CDMA each channel occupies the whole band. In the example that was cited before, the carrier had a rate of 1.23 Mbps. The pseudo random code repeated every $2^{15} - 1 = 32,767$ chips. With this length code, 64 orthogonal channels can be obtained that are sufficiently orthogonal so that they will not interfere with each other when decoded. Usually, the code for each of the 64 channels is a time shift of the previous code. This eases the synchronization and acquisition problem in CDMA.

There is another CDMA system that spreads the signal even more than normal CDMA. This is called broadband CDMA and typically spreads the signal over about 5 MHz. The additional spreading allows the service to be overlaid on top of an existing service. Proponents of wide band

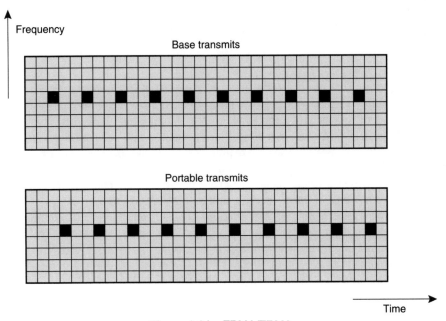

Figure 2.21 FDMA/TDMA.

CDMA claim that the spreading lowers the spectral energy to such a degree that the incumbent in that frequency band does not notice the presence of the broadband CDMA signal. Two such systems are proposed for PCS standards as we will discuss in a later chapter.

The comparison between TDMA and CDMA has received much attention. The two technologies are competing head to head, and much investment is on the line. The differences can be summarized as follows:

- TDMA
  - Simple to implement
  - Traditional
  - Can increase spectrum utilization with power control
- CDMA
  - Requires complex processing
  - Has been integrated into high power chips
  - Claims high spectral efficiency
  - Requires fast power control to achieve efficiency.

Early implementations of CDMA have proven difficult. This is to be expected from a new technology, especially one as complex as CDMA. It may not be successful the first time out of the gate; however, it cannot be counted out because it is theoretically very strong. We will discuss this later in much greater detail.

Cellularization Principles

Given a range of frequencies, a modulation scheme, and a multiplexing scheme, we have a number of total channels. Next, we must cover the service area with cells through which the users can roam. The cellular network connects the roaming user with the fixed network as shown in Figure 2.22. The total number of channels is divided among the cells in such a way so that adjacent cells do not use the same set of channels. The channels are used by nonadjacent cells some distance away. The main source of interference in cellular networks is the interference of other cellular users. In other words, the main source of interference is self-interference. Therefore, the choice of cell repeating pattern is a crucial decision. It is a trade-off between the amount of interference introduced, and the number of channels available in each cell.

Cells can range in size from 30 to 40 Km in rural areas to 1 Km or less in urban areas. The smaller cells can be overlaid on top of the larger cells as shown in Figure 2.23.

Designing a cellular network is similar to coloring a map in such a way that no two adjacent states have the same color. The repeating patterns can be 3, 4, 7, 12, or multiples. The most com-

Airlink Network

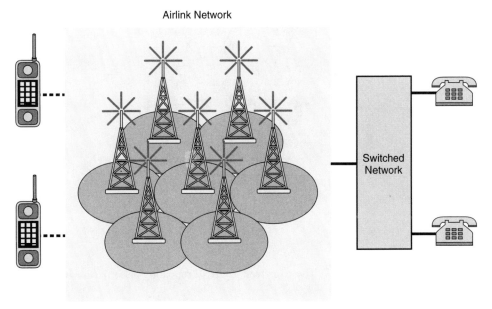

Figure 2.22   Cellular network.

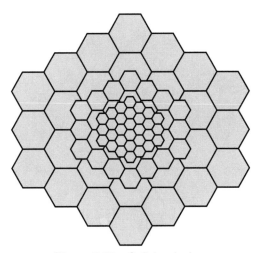

Figure 2.23   Cellular design.

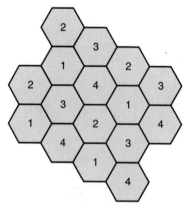

Figure 2.24   Four-cell repeating pattern.

mon repeating patterns are 4 and 7. These, as well as the 12 repeating patterns are shown in Figures 2.24 through 2.26.

The trade-off between repeating number K and the level of interference depends on the D/R ratio illustrated in Figure 2.27. This ratio is given by:

$$Q = D/R = (3K)^{1/2}. \tag{2.16}$$

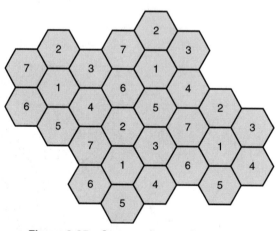

Figure 2.25   Seven-cell repeating pattern.

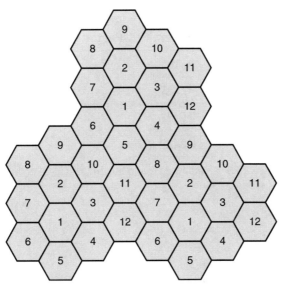

Figure 2.26 Twelve-cell repeating pattern.

As K increases,

- The number of channels per cell falls
- The frequency reuse factor Q increases
- Interference decreases.

An optimum is obtained depending on the system under consideration. The major digital cellular choices of parameters is shown in Figure 2.28. AMPS and TDMA use the same reuse factor since TDMA is based on AMPS. CDMA reuses the same frequency spectrum in adjacent cells. How this works will be discussed in detail in a later chapter.

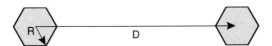

Figure 2.27 Frequency reuse factor: D/R ratio.

System	Reuse Factor
AMPS	7
GSM	4
TDMA	7
CDMA	1

Figure 2.28   Frequency reuse factors for digital cellular.

Summary

In this chapter we have laid down the foundation for cellular systems. We have developed propagation formulas starting from intuitive ideas. We discussed the basic interactions of frequency and cell size and power and their impact on the application of systems such TDMA, CDMA, GSM, and DCS to rural and urban areas. We presented alternative modulation techniques and discussed their merits. We outlined source coding methods for voice and data, and talked about error detection and correction, as well as security coding. We described multiple access techniques and compared them including the controversial comparison between TDMA and CDMA. Finally, we presented the basics of cellularization principles and showed the choices made by the major digital cellular systems. Next, we will discuss specific cellular systems, both analog and digital.

3 Cellular Technologies

Analog cellular has been serving mobile professionals for a number of years. The ramp in demand brought about the evolution to digital cellular. In this chapter, we first present the background of analog cellular, then we discuss the major digital cellular technologies and compare them. Finally, we present an overview of satellite communications systems and discuss how they fit in with cellular:

- Analog cellular systems
  - Advanced Mobile Phone System (AMPS)
  - Nordic Mobile Telephone (NMT)
  - Total Access Communications System (TACS)
- Digital cellular systems
  - U.S. Digital Cellular (USDC): TDMA, CDMA
  - Global System Mobile (GSM)
  - Digital Cordless System (DCS 1800)
  - Japanese Digital Cellular (PDC)
- Satellite systems
  - GEO
  - LEO
  - MEO
  - HEO.

In this chapter, we focus on the cellular part of Figure 3.1, and end the chapter with an overview of the satellite part. Cell sizes vary over a large range for cellular services, from less than 1 Km to more than 30 Km. Satellite cell sizes can be thousands of Km or even larger in size. The data rates available with cellular are on the order of 10 Kbps, the same is true with satellites.

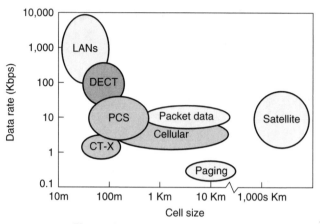

Figure 3.1   Network positioning.

First Generation Cellular

First generation cellular systems are analog. They use analog frequency modulation for the voice, and digital Frequency Shift Keying for signaling. They use straightforward FDMA for channel access. The cell sizes range from 0.5 Km to 10 Km, and they provide handover from one cell to another. They also provide roaming from one service provider to another. The major analog cellular systems, and where they are used is shown below:

- Americas
  - AMPS
- Europe
  - NMT all over Europe
  - TACS in United Kingdom, Italy, Austria, Spain, and Ireland
  - C 450 in Germany and Portugal
  - Radiocom 2000 in France
  - RTMS in Italy
- Japan
  - NTT system
  - IDO system
  - DDI Cellular group

- Asia, Africa, Australia, and other parts of the world
  - AMPS
  - NMT
  - TACS.

In the United States, cellular was first authorized by the FCC in 1982. The first system went on the air in October of 1983 in Chicago. It took four years until October of 1987 to reach 1 million customers on the air. Now there are over 20 million customers. The cumulative capital investment to serve 20 million customers is about $18 billion, or about $900 per customer.

Figure 3.2 depicts the power levels and ranges possible with AMPS analog cellular in the United States. The car-mounted units can transmit up to 3 watts and can be up to 15 miles away from the base station. Hand-held units can transmit up to 0.6 watts and be up to 5 miles away from the base station.

In each metropolitan area there can be up to two cellular providers. Each provider is allocated 25 MHz. Each voice channel is a pair of channels 30 KHz wide. With 25 MHz, this gives each service provider a total of 416 duplex voice channels. AMPS uses a seven-cell repeating pattern; therefore, those 416 channels must be divided among 7 cells. Each cell then has about 60 voice channels to serve the customers in that cell. The base transmits in the range of 869 to 894 MHz. The mobile transmits in the range of 824 to 849 MHz. The voice uses FM analog modulation. The signaling uses 10 Kbps digital FSK modulation. The MAC is FDMA, and the duplexing method is Frequency Division Duplexing. That means that one frequency range is used in one direction, and another frequency range is used in the other direction. Besides FDD, the other duplexing method is Time Division Duplexing that is most commonly used with cordless systems. TDD utilizes two time slots, one for each direction.

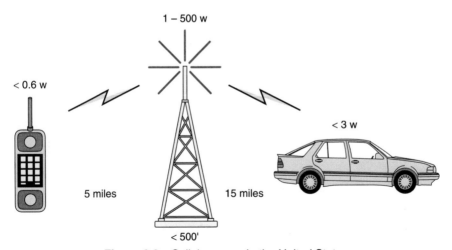

Figure 3.2   Cellular range in the United States.

Nordic Mobile Telephone has two systems at two frequency bands:

- NMT 900 has 2,000 channels in the 900 MHz band
- NMT 450 has only 180 channels in the 450 MHz band.

As the name implies, NMT is used, in particular, in the Nordic countries. NMT 450 is especially useful in sparsely populated areas. The low frequency of 450 MHz allows it to cover large areas with little transmitted power. NMT has channels that are 25-KHz wide. It provides full roaming and uses in-band signaling.

Total Access Communications System is based on AMPS. It operates in the 900-MHz band. The channels are 25-KHz wide. It provides full roaming and uses out-of-band signaling. TACS has high-peak frequency deviation in its analog FM modulation of voice and, therefore, good fidelity. Twenty channels are dedicated for out-of-band signaling; it is highly redundant. The signals are repeated five times and protected by a block code. During handover, when transmission quality is poorest, signals are repeated 11 times. It differs from AMPS in the following ways:

- 25-KHz channels instead of 30 KHz
- Higher voice quality due to the higher modulation index
- Greater resistance to noise and interference.

Enhanced TACS provide greater capacity over TACS through an additional 66 MHz of bandwidth. The two bands are:

- TACS bands
  - 890–915 MHz uplink
  - 935–960 MHz downlink
- E-TACS
  - 962–905 MHz uplink
  - 917–950 MHz downlink.

The European spectrum for cellular is depicted in Figure 3.3 along with other services. The analog systems are at 900 MHz with the exception of NMT that is at 450 MHz. GSM is at 900 MHz. Smaller cell systems such as DCS 1800 and DECT are just below 2 GHz. To put these allocations in perspective, the figure shows that paging and some data networks are at lower frequencies all the way down to 87 MHz. The installed base of analog cellular systems in Europe is shown in Figure 3.4.

In Japan, there is a total of 56 MHz allocated. NTT was the first system and went into service in Tokyo in 1979. It contains 600 duplex channels each 25-KHz wide. Signaling was initially at 300 bps. In 1988, the system was enhanced as follows:

- The channel spacing was dropped to 12.5 KHz with interleaving
- The signaling rate was increased to 2,400 bps
- A 100 bps associated control channel was introduced.

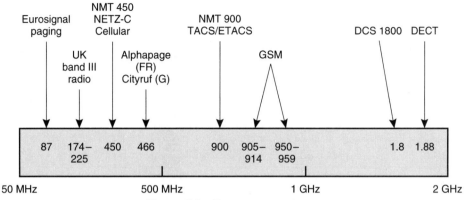

Figure 3.3   European spectrum.

System	Million users
TACS	3.7
NMT	2.9
C-450	0.9

Figure 3.4   Installed base of analog cellular in Europe.

In 1987, two additional carriers were allowed in Japan. IDO introduced service in the Kanto–Tokaido areas using the NTT high capacity system. DDI Cellular Group provided service outside metropolitan areas using JTACS/NTACS that are based on TACS. IDO and DDI have formed partnerships to allow nationwide roaming. There are about 2.6 million users of analog cellular in Japan.

Figure 3.5 compares the capacities of analog cellular systems worldwide.

Digital Cellular

Spurred by demand by demand in the United States, and the need to have a Pan European system in Europe, the cellular industry moved to digital technology. In the United States, analog cellular systems were running out of capacity in major metropolitan areas such as Los Angeles and New York.

Region	Standard	Frequency, MHz	BW, MHz	Channels
Americas	AMPS	924-849/869-894	50	832
Europe	TACS	890-915/935-960	50	1,000
United Kingdom	E-TACS	872-905/917-950	66	1,240
Europe	NMT 450	453-457/463-467	9	180
Europe	NMT 900	890-915/935-960	50	1,999
Germany	C450	450-456/460-466	12	573
Italy	RTMS	450-455/460-465	10	200
France	Radiocom	200, 400	35	1,712
Japan	NTT	200, 400	50	1,640
Japan	JTACS/NTACS	900	33	800

Figure 3.5 Analog cellular capacities worldwide.

The standards bodies, in particular TR45 addressed the problem by formulating what became the IS54 digital TDMA standard. In Europe, ETSI developed GSM. The major impetus for that work was to allow people to be able to roam within Europe. GSM now is one of the most popularly implemented standards worldwide.

The technological advantages of digital over analog are that digital:

- Accommodates more powerful digital speech coding techniques
- Offers improved spectral efficiency
- Can provide better speech quality
- Can handle data more easily
- Can provide digital encryption easily.

Without powerful speech coding techniques, digital would not be able to provide the improved spectral efficiency needed to increase the number of channels over analog. AMPS uses 30 KHz per voice channel with analog FM modulation for voice. Digital TDMA derives three channels from one channel by digitally coding the voice down to 8 Kbps. Without the low coding rate, the capacity of digital TDMA would not be much larger than the capacity of analog AMPS.

The quality of speech of analog versus digital is a subjective issue. The impairments are of a different nature. In analog circuits, as the quality degrades, noise increases, until the voice is no longer intelligible, and the signal is too weak to maintain the connection. With digital circuits, the quality of the voice remains fairly constant until the connection can no longer be maintained. The quality of the voice even under ideal circuit conditions is determined by the coding technique. There are many techniques as discussed in a previous chapter. As time goes on, the quality will go up, and the rates will go down. Most people would say that the quality of the 8 Kbps systems in digital TDMA and the 13-Kbps systems in GSM are good.

Since data starts out as digital, one would expect digital systems to handle data more expeditiously. This will eventually be true. At the present time, we can actually get a higher data rate from an analog cellular circuit than we can from a digital circuit. The reason for this is that cellular systems are optimized for voice at the present time and require special equipment and signals to handle data. Analog cellular leveraged the great advances in wired network modem technology. Analog modems for the wired network are approaching Shanon's Theorem of maximum throughput. They are now providing 28.8 Kbps over an analog wired telephone circuit. Analog cellular modems within the span of a few years have come close to that. Analog cellular modems can provide up to 14.4 Kbps without compression over an analog cellular circuit, and they are not very expensive, perhaps in the range of $300 for a PCMCIA model that easily fits inside a notebook computer or a Personal Digital Assistant.

To send data through a digital cellular circuit, we have to live with the current limit of the channel definition that is optimized for voice. This limits the maximum data rate to 9.6 Kbps today and represents the equivalent of one voice circuit at the nominal vocoding rate. To overcome this, we have to allow data circuits to use the available bandwidth more freely. Some companies are already experimenting with putting together several equivalent voice circuits together to increase the possible data rate by a factor of 2, 3, or more up to the maximum rate possible per carrier.

The last advantage of digital over analog cellular delineated above is the ease with which encryption can be included in digital cellular. This goes without argument. Encryption techniques are inherently digital, and lend themselves naturally to a signal that is already digital. One of the greatest contributions of digital cellular is in fact better security, both privacy of the data as well as a much more secure authentication process to greatly reduce the rampant problem of cellular fraud.

The digital cellular bands in North America, Europe, and Japan are shown in relative scale in Figure 3.6. There is a total of 50 MHz allocated in North America. In Europe, the initial allocation is also 50 MHz with another 20 for future allocation. In Japan there is a total of 80 MHz. The up-frequency band is always the lower band in order to ease the power requirements for the portable. The standards developed in North America are Digital TDMA IS 54/136, and Digital CDMA IS 95. The standard developed in Europe for this band is GSM 900. The standard developed in Japan is PDC. These standards will be discussed shortly. We expect that the standards that were developed in each region will predominate in that region. We also expect those standards to be offered and to have varying degrees of success in other regions. The most notable example is GSM that is finding great acceptance throughout the world. We also expect TDMA and CDMA to be aggressively offered throughout the world, and PDC to be offered throughout the world particularly in parts of Asia.

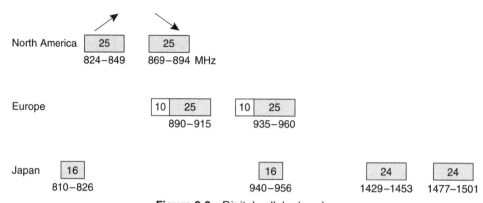

Figure 3.6 Digital cellular bands.

TDMA Digital Cellular

In 1990, the Telecommunications Industry Association in the United States approved IS 54. From its inception, IS 54, or TDMA was designed to be dual-mode analog and digital. This means that the base stations can operate on both systems and accommodate both analog as well as digital handsets. The handsets can also be dual mode. This allows a user to roam from an area with old analog-only base stations to an area with a dual-mode base station, and switch to the more efficient digital system while maintaining the call. This dual-mode operation is advantageous in a country like the United States, because there are widely varying densities of populations across the country. In certain parts of the Midwest, analog cellular is a good solution for many years to come due to the light population density. In the more congested urban areas, the more efficient digital standard is required to handle the burgeoning demand.

In contrast, GSM is digital only. Europe generally has more uniform population densities, with notable exceptions in the Nordic countries and in parts of Eastern Europe. With GSM, a service provider has to offer either the digital service, or the older analog service to his customers. If a customer requires both services because he works in areas that are served by one or the other, he must either have two separate handsets, or a combined handset if one is manufactured. Not many manufacturers offer combined handsets for analog and digital cellular in Europe, because the installed base of analog cellular in Europe is not huge, so the demand for such a unit does not justify the development.

TDMA IS 54 triples the capacity of analog AMPS by deriving three channels from each 30-KHz carrier. This is based on 8 Kbps voice coding. With half-rate codecs running at 4 Kbps, the capacity can be further doubled to be six times that of AMPS. IS54 is, strictly speaking, FDMA/TDMA, since it uses the FDMA structure of AMPS and then overlays the three channel per carrier TDMA system on top. The basic parameters of IS 54 can be summarized as follows:

- 50 MHz total allocation per geographical area
- Two service providers in each region, each with 25 MHz

- Frequency Division Duplexing, thereby 12.5 MHz in each direction
- 30-KHz carriers
- 416 carriers in each direction
- Each carrier provides 3 TDMA channels
- A total of 1,248 channels in each direction per service provider
- A cell-repeating pattern of seven
- 178 full duplex channels per cell.

We will use this data later to develop an example of applying TDMA to a sample city. The other major parameters of TDMA are:

- The raw bit rate of each carrier is 48.6 Kbps
- The modulation is $\pi/4$ DQPSK running at 24.3 Kbaud
- Voice is coded using Vector Sum Excited Linear Predictive coding running at 7.95 Kbps
- Adaptive equalization is used to mitigate Inter Symbol Interference.

Each vocoded voice channel uses about 8 Kbps. With error detection and correction, signaling, and other overhead, the total data rate required is almost 50 Kbps. We will find this kind of overhead is typical with most cellular systems. Since the available bandwidth per carrier is only 30 KHz, we have to use higher-order modulation than binary. The choice is QPSK which provides two bits per sample. In addition, differential Quadrature Phase Shift Keying (QPSK) is chosen to ease the phase stability requirement of the receiver. With Differential Quadrature Phase Shift Keying (DQPSK), the information is in the difference of the phase of two successive samples rather than in the absolute phase, so the phase can drift slightly from one sample to the next and the information remains intact. Finally, the $\pi/4$ is a way of changing the phase smoothly in order to have a spectrum that is contained within the allocated spectrum mask.

At 24.3 Kbaud, the baud length is about 41 microseconds. A path length difference of 1 Km would cause a delay of about 3 microseconds. Such a delay is a small fraction of a baud length and should actually improve the received signal and not cause intersymbol interference. Path lengths greater than 1 Km would mean that the received reflection is of sufficiently low amplitude and does not have much of an effect. Nevertheless TDMA incorporates adaptive equalization to further improve the situation.

IS 54 uses the AMPS control channel running at 10 Kbps for signaling. IS 136 that replaces IS 54 provides 48.6 Kbps signaling rate. With this rate, several exciting new features are possible:

- Point-to-point short messaging
- Broadcast messaging
- Group addressing

- Private user groups
- Slotted paging channels.

Some of these features such as point-to-point short messaging, private user groups, and the slotted paging channels are part of GSM. The short messaging is akin to two-way paging. The maximum message length is limited, so it is not suited to general bursty traffic applications, but it does provide an excellent two-way advanced paging capability. This feature is particularly useful when combined with voice mail and fax. The short messages are used to notify the user that he has a voice message or a fax waiting. The voice message could have been received while the user's handset was turned off or the user was out of range. When the set is off or the user is out of range, the call is typically forwarded to voice mail. This service is often provided with no additional cost to the cellular user.

Broadcast messaging and group addressing is useful when working with groups of people or departments where certain information needs to be known by the whole group. Private user groups are a way of providing virtual private networks within the public infrastructure. When one member of the closed user group calls another member, the charge is less than when the call is to someone outside the group. In fact, the charge could be a flat monthly charge with unlimited calling within the user group. This is an important trend that allows the sharing of infrastructure for public and private networks.

Slotted paging channels are a feature that helps reduce battery drain. A paging channel is part of the signaling structure of IS 136. Cellular systems require a means of notifying a customer that he has a call coming; this is done over a so-called paging channel. However, this channel is not for customer paging traffic; it is a signal to notify the customer of an incoming call. When the handset is turned on but not actively on a call, it is in the idle mode. While it is in this mode, it is performing several functions, including waiting for a possible incoming call. A slotted paging channel means that the notification of an incoming call comes at a specific predefined slot in time. This allows the handset to sleep until this predefined time slot, wake up just then to see if a call is coming, and if not, go back to sleep until the next such slot.

The last part of the digital TDMA standard is IS 41. IS 41 provides the details for service providers to allow customers to roam among them. It is the mechanism for sending the customer information from one service provider to another. Consequently, the new service provider can deliver calls to the customer, provide him with the services he has signed up for, and bill him accordingly. Taken together, IS 136 and IS 41 form the complete standard. GSM provides both those parts in a single standard.

CDMA Digital Cellular

This highly visible standard was first proposed by Qualcomm. It was coolly received at first. It was a technology that was new to the telecommunications industry. It seemed overly complex, and it was untried. One of the main people behind CDMA is Andrew Viterbi. He is a brilliant Italian mathematician who is responsible for many of the sophisticated error detection and correction codes we use.

The basic argument behind CDMA is that the information signal modulates a noiselike carrier, the pseudo random code, and hence is a very efficient user of the available bandwidth as predicted by Shanon's information Theorem. This becomes especially important in very dense applications such as in certain cities in Asia. And in fact, CDMA is implemented in Hong Kong and other cities.

To convince the industry that CDMA was viable, Qualcomm built a trial system in San Diego and reported successes in the critical parts of the system. They claim 10 times the frequency efficiency of AMPS as contrasted with a three-times advantage of TDMA. This, however, has not been shown in a large scale implementation. Some of the critical challenges of CDMA include:

- All users in a given cell are transmitting at the same time in the same frequency band. Can they be made not to interfere with each other? In particular, will a user who is near the base station saturate the base station altogether so that it cannot receive users who are farther away?

- CDMA claims a reuse factor of one. This means that the same frequencies can be used in adjacent cells. Can the codes provide sufficient separation for this to work in real life situations?

- The pseudo random codes are long: the processing needed to code and decode them are complex. Can such complexity be built into a battery-powered small handset economically?

- CDMA claims soft handover. This means that a moving user can receive two, or sometimes more than two base stations at the same time, combine the signals together, and make the handover in a soft manner instead of suddenly as in other systems. Will this place an unmanageable burden on the base stations, because in essence they would have to handle a great increase in additional traffic?

- CDMA uses the sophisticated method of rake filtering to take advantage of multipath in a constructive way. It looks for the reflections and constructively combines them with the strongest received signal. This is an excellent way of dealing with multipath, but can its complexity be cost-effectively implemented in the small, battery-powered handsets?

These, and other questions are being asked of the CDMA proponents. Only a successful large-scale implementation can answer these questions satisfactorily. One thing can be said without the trials. Even if CDMA does not become widely implemented at first, its theoretical roots are so strong that it is certain to emerge at a later time and be a great success.

Now let us take a look at how CDMA works and how it deals with each of the above challenges. CDMA uses Frequency Division Duplexing like TDMA. Each direction of transmission uses a 1.23-MHz band. Within this band, a single carrier serves all users. The chip rate on this carrier is 1.2288 Mcps using simple bipolar PSK. The parameters of the system are:

- 8 Kbps vocoding rate initially. Future 4, 2, and even 1 Kbps rates are envisioned
- With error detection and correction, this rate becomes 19.2 Kbps per channel
- Interleaving of the data allows error correction to be more effective

- The pseudo random code is $2^{15} - 1 = 32,767$ chips long
- Walsh codes provide 64 orthogonal channels
- Short codes provide differentiation among cell sites.

In essence, the short codes require that the pseudo random codes support another level of coding. Whether this much coding can be made orthogonal in an actual situation from a code that is 32,767 chips long remains to seen in a large scale implementation.

The base station block diagram for each channel is shown in Figure 3.7. The input signal is 9.6 Kbps. With EDC, this becomes 19.2 Kbps. Interleaving takes place next, not affecting the data rate. Next, the signal is convolved with the long code resulting in the 1.2288-Mcps stream. The Walsh codes are applied to yield the 64 orthogonal channels, and finally the short codes are applied to provide cell site differentiation. The resulting 1.2288-Mcps signal is sent out for each channel.

The picture for multiple channels is shown in Figure 3.8. Channel number zero is a reserve for the pilot channel and Channel 32 is used for the synchronization channel. Channels 1 through 7 are used for signaling; the remaining 55 channels are used for traffic. Each channel is weighted so it arrives at the handset with sufficient power but no more. This helps reduce overall interference on the air.

When a handset is first turned on, it searches for a pilot signal. If it finds more than one, it picks the strongest one and synchronizes to it. It then registers with that base station so it can receive calls. The base station alerts the handset of an incoming call on a signaling channel. When the mobile initiates a call, it requests a channel from the base station. If that request collides with a request from another mobile, the mobile waits a random time and tries again. The base station then assigns the mobile a channel using one of the Walsh codes.

At 1.2288 Mcps, the chip length is about 250 meters. Path lengths that are a significant fraction of 250 meters are common outdoors but can even occur indoors. Rake filtering uses a filter

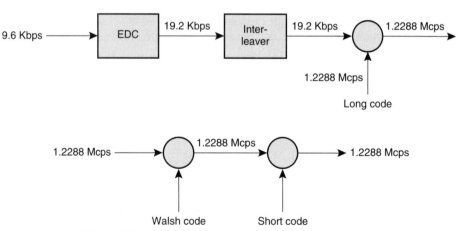

Figure 3.7   CDMA base station transmitter per channel.

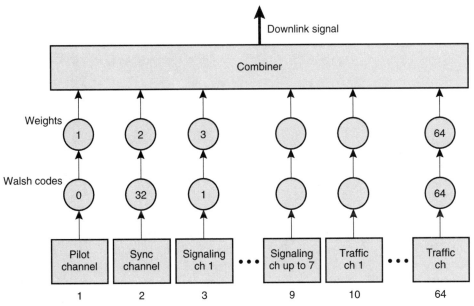

Figure 3.8 CDMA base station transmitter.

matched to the impulse response of the signal to search for reflections of the signal. The first signal received is delayed and is combined with these reflections in a constructive way to enhance the total received signal.

When a mobile detects a second base station, it requests a second Walsh code from the new base station, and treats the second signal as if it were multipath to combine it with the main received signal using the rake filter and all of its reflections. It continues in this way until it is time to deregister with the old base station and register with the new base station. This is soft hand-off.

To deal with the problem of a mobile near the base station that is saturating the base so it cannot hear other distant mobiles, agile power control is used. The situation is illustrated in Figure 3.9. There is one user near the base station, and one at the edge of the coverage area. The mobile performs agile power control in two steps:

- Open loop control—where the mobile determines the distance from the base, from other signals received from it and approximately adjusts its transmitted power
- Closed loop control—where after receiving signals from that mobile, the base more precisely instructs how to adjust its transmitted power.

The goal of agile power control is to have all the powers from all the mobiles in the coverage area be about equal no matter how far each of them is from the base station. This is required to achieve the capacity efficiency of CDMA. It is, in general, a good idea to reduce the power transmitted on

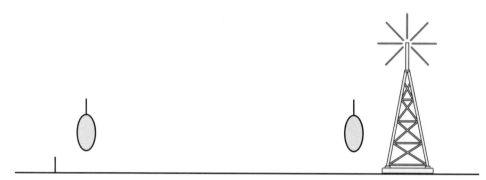

Figure 3.9   The near-far problem.

the air to the absolute minimum required for good reception—the less power transmitted, the less potential interference with other users. TDMA systems are being looked at to see if their efficiency can be improved through power control, and the answer seems to be, yes. In addition, such power control saves battery life in the mobile. GSM performs such power control in a simple way with the primary purpose of saving battery life. The inherent spectrum savings achieved by this is not explicitly taken advantage of. The stated spectrum efficiency of GSM is below that stated for even digital TDMA and is probably conservative.

Inter Digital in cooperation with Oki Electronics has experimented with a system that spreads the signal even further than CDMA. It is referred to as broadband CDMA and uses about 5 MHz. The broad spreading is used for two purposes:

- Code Division Multiple Access
- Overlaying of existing primary users in the spectrum.

The signal spectral energy is so low that it does not interfere with an existing primary user of the spectrum. This means that such a broadband CDMA system can overlay an existing analog cellular or even a digital cellular system. This is the idea used by wireless LANs and other spread spectrum systems.

Comparison of TDMA and CDMA

This discussion will ultimately have to be settled in the marketplace in large scale implementation. The basic arguments for each side are summarized by:

- TDMA
  - Simple to implement

- Traditional solution
- Possible greater spectrum efficiency through power control
- CDMA
  - Complex processing
  - Integrated into high-power chips
  - Potential high-spectrum utilization efficiency
  - Fast-power control to achieve efficiency.

The argument of tradition and simplicity may not seem important, but it has been an issue. A simple and tried solution is often preferred by a large number of people. The cost and complexity of CDMA can disappear once volume has been established and the components have been put to the test of use.

Early implementations of CDMA may find the reuse factor of one difficult to implement. The levels of coding may be too much for the length of code chosen to ensure adequate orthogonality. This may force the early implementors to use the reuse factor of seven that is used by the underlying AMPS standard. This would negate one of the major advantages of CDMA of providing greater bandwidth efficiency.

Another challenge that may be difficult to overcome initially is soft handoff. Cell designs, especially in downtown areas with large buildings and other obstructions have many areas of overlap. Whenever there is an area of overlap, a CDMA system would provide coverage from the base stations covering the overlap area. In essence, this means that the base stations are handling duplicate traffic. The amount of duplicate traffic increases as the areas of overlap increase. This could easily double the amount of traffic handled by the base stations and force early implementors to turn off soft handoff.

GSM

In 1982, the Conference of European PTs (CEPT) established what was then called Group Speciale Mobile. Its original intent was to develop a Pan European cellular system to allow Europeans to roam from one country to another with a single mobile. Now GSM stands for Global System for Mobile Communications and seems to be living up to its new name. It is being adopted by more countries than any other digital cellular standard. Seven years later, European Telecommunications Standards Institute (ETSI) formed a GSM technical committee. Phase 1 of the standard is now complete and comprises more than 161 documents and 6,000 pages. It is comprehensive and includes both the areas covered by IS 136 as well as IS 41 for interconnection among different service providers.

GSM is aimed at the 900 MHz band. Its companion DCS 1800 is for the 1.8-GHz band. GSM and DCS are almost the same. The major differences are the frequency band and the power levels. This will be covered in the next chapter which deals with GSM in detail. GSM is digital only, not dual mode such as IS 136.

GSM services are summarized below:

- International roaming
- Good speech quality
- Ability to support hand-helds
- Aims toward ISDN capabilities
- Data
  - 300–9600 bps
  - Asynchronous and synchronous
  - Circuit-switched and interface to packet-switched networks
- Group 3 fax
- Messaging services
  - Short Message Service Point to Point (SMSPP)
  - Short Message Service Cell Broadcast (SMSCB).

The GSM allocations fall within the bands recommended by the World Association of Radio Communications (WARC) as shown in Figure 3.10. WARC does not allocate spectrum in any given country. The purpose of their recommendations is to allow for harmonizations of allocations made by the specific regulatory agencies of different countries such as CEPT, the FCC, and MPT so that there is good possibility for a user to take his or her handset from one country to another and continue to use it. The frequency allocations may not be exactly the same, but they can be close enough so that the handset can be built to tune to the slightly different frequencies. There will be much more detail about GSM in the next chapter. Now let us take a look at the digital cellular system in Japan.

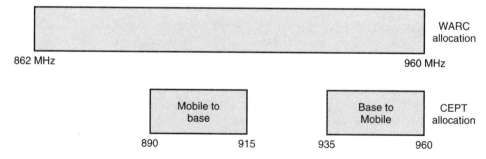

Figure 3.10 GSM allocation relative to the WARC recommendation.

Personal Digital Cellular in Japan

There are two types of analog cellular systems in Japan:

- NTT
- JTACS.

In 1991, MPT established a new digital cellular standard in Japan. It was named Personal Digital Cellular or PDC. It is very similar to IS 54 with a major difference of having 25-KHz spacing instead of 30 KHz. The parameters of PDC are:

- Total of 80 MHz allocated
- 810–826/940–956 MHz
- 1429–1453/1477–1501 MHz
- Reuse factor of 4
- 42 Kbps data rate for each carrier
- $\pi/4$ DQPSK
- 6.7 Kbps VSELP voice coding
- With error detection and correction, the rate per channel is 11.2 Kbps
- Supports group 3 fax
- Provides 4.8 Kbps data with MNP

There are 5 PDC operators in Japan. PDC is very popular, because it is perceived to have high quality, high security, and the handsets have longer battery life than their analog counterparts.

Comparison of Digital Cellular Standards

Figure 3.11 compares the major digital cellular standards discussed so far. They are all FDMA/TDMA with the exception of CDMA. The carrier spacing varies greatly among the systems. IS 54 uses the AMPS spacing as does PDC. GSM uses a larger spacing as a trade-off between multiplexing number and overall data rate that makes it susceptible to multipath. The channels per carrier also vary greatly between GSM, CDMA and the AMPS-based standards. We will take a look at the efficiency of the various systems shortly. The modulation is mostly PSK. It is simple bipolar PSK for CDMA, DQPSK for IS 54 and PDC, and GMSK (a form of FSK for GSM).

Figure 3.12 compares the bandwidth per channel for the different digital cellular standards. AMPS is used as the reference. It has one FDMA channel per 30-KHz carrier. The reuse factor is

Standard	MAC	Carrier BW	Channels/carrier	Modulation
GSM	FDMA/TDMA	200 KHz	8 (16)	GMSK
IS54	FDMA/TDMA	30 KHz	3 (6)	π/4 DQPSK
IS95	CDMA	1.23 MHz	64 (128)	BPSK
PDC	FDMA/TDMA	25 KHz	3 (6)	π/4 DQPSK

Figure 3.11   Digital cellular standards.

System	BW/carrier	Channels	Reuse factor	BW/channel
AMPS	30 KHz	1	7	210 KHz
TDMA	30 KHz	3	7	70 KHz
GSM	200 KHz	8	4	100 KHz
CDMA	1.23 MHz	64	1	19.3 KHz

Figure 3.12   Bandwidth per channel comparison.

seven, so the effective bandwidth per voice channel is 210 KHz. TDMA triples that. GSM has eight channels for each 200-KHz carrier. Its reuse factor is four, so its effective bandwidth per carrier is 100 KHz, a little less than TDMA. As mentioned before, the efficiency of GSM may be better than stated because of such features as power control and other features that are discussed in the next chapter. These factors are not taken advantage of explicitly. CDMA claims a bandwidth per channel that makes it more than 10 times more efficient than AMPS. This is based on a reuse factor of one; this means that all 64 Walsh codes can be reused from one cell to the other, even an adjacent one.

A Sample City

Suppose that we want to build a cellular system for a city such as San Francisco. Here are the basic parameters:

- Population of about 500,000 people
- Area of about 120 square Km

- Cell radius of 1 Km
- Cellular penetration = 10 percent
  - 50,000 cellular phones in city
- Cellular phone density
  - 417 phones per Km^2
  - 1,309 phones per cell
- Each person speaks 5 percent in the busy hour
- Total of 65 Erlangs per cell
- Need 70 channels in each cell to achieve 5 percent blocking.

A cell radius of 1 Km is reasonable for a city with the density of San Francisco. For a denser city we may use a smaller cell. In fact, in the heavily populated downtown area of San Francisco, we may use smaller cells and larger cells in the outer parts. Suppose the average is about 1 Km and the cellular penetration is about 10 percent. This means that one out of 10 people has a cellular phone. The assumption that each person speaks 5 percent of the time may be light, but it is a typical parameter that cellular service providers use. It is somewhat sensitive to the cost of the service based on the amount of time a user speaks during the busy hour—the hour during which the demand is expected to be the highest. Telephone systems are designed to meet a certain blocking probability for such a busy hour. A 5 percent usage is about three minutes in the busy hour that may be one average length call or perhaps two shorter calls.

An Erlang is a measure of traffic and is equivalent to one person talking the whole hour. The 70 required channels is obtained from traffic tables for an Erlang B arrival process. It is typically used for engineering of such systems. The result is a requirement of 70 channels to provide a 5 percent grade of service. This means that 5 percent of the time when we want a channel, we will get an all-circuits busy signal. This does not mean that the person we are calling is busy, but rather that all the channels in the cell we are in are busy, so we cannot get out to reach anyone.

To put this into perspective—the wired telephone network is nominally designed to meet a blocking criterion of 1 percent. This means that 1 percent of the time when we lift the receiver, we will get an all-lines busy signal, or when we attempt to make a call to a specific region of the country, we may get an all-trunks busy signal. We all have had experience with this, and in most cases, personal experience reflects a much lower blocking percentage than 1 percent. Most of the wired phone network is designed quite conservatively with a great deal of spare capacity even when the traffic is heavy. The isolated cases when we do run into an all-lines or all-trunks busy signal are very unusual cases, for instance, mother's day, or perhaps some sort of emergency taking place such as a severe storm or an earthquake.

This may not be the situation for cellular systems. Since the bandwidth and capacity come at a much greater cost, the blocking experienced by users may be very noticeable and an issue as the demand rises.

Now let us suppose that we want to serve San Francisco with TDMA cellular. The basic parameters are:

- Total bandwidth available = 50 MHz
- Each carrier uses 30 KHz
- FDD
- Each carrier provides 3 TDMA channels
- Total number of duplex channels = 2,496 full duplex channels
- Reuse factor = seven
- 356 channels per cell
- 70 channels required for San Francisco per 1 Km radius cell
- Can serve city of San Francisco with a 5 to 7 density.

The 50 MHz bandwidth is the total bandwidth available. It is actually divided between two service providers. Having two service providers creates healthy competition; however, it causes traffic inefficiency due to the effect of trunk group splintering. We are ignoring this effect at this time. Its magnitude will be discussed in a later chapter.

The total number of channels per cell assuming one service provider is 356. We require 70 channels to serve San Francisco with 10 percent penetration. This means that we can serve San Francisco with five times the penetration, or 50 percent of the population, which is quite heavy. Or it is easy to imagine serving a city with five times the density of San Francisco. Consider, for example, an Asian city such as Hong Kong. We could also use larger cells in San Francisco at least initially, and then make the cell sizes smaller as the penetration increases, particularly in the denser financial district. All these are options. The example serves to set a reference point to see what is possible with a system such as TDMA.

Cellular Supply Strategies

The key elements of the supply chain for cellular services is shown in Figure 3.13. The subsystem manufacturers provide chip sets, and other subsystems that go into the infrastructure of switching equipment and base station hardware and software. The mobile network operators build out the networks and provide air time to service providers who put packages together for the end users possibly along with a terminal. The possibilities are many.

The key elements of the supply chain that are taking place and evolving over time are:

- Competitive network operators
- Network operators multisourcing equipment manufacturers
- Introduction of service providers

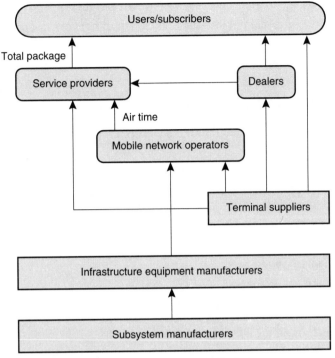

Figure 3.13 Cellular supply chain.

- Intense competition for terminal supplies
- Emerging joint ventures.

In Europe, in the area of infrastructure, Ericsson is a leader. With GSM, Siemens is establishing a strong role. Motorola, Alcatel, Phillips, and Nokia are gaining good market position. In the area of terminal supply, Motorola and Nokia dominate the market. Challengers are Ericsson, NEC, Panasonic, Phillips, Siemens and others. In the area of network operations, national suppliers, or nationally led consortiums are the dominant force. In the area of distribution systems, the United Kingdom developed the concept of service providers. This concept is catching on in other countries including Germany and France.

The key questions facing suppliers are:

- Whether or not to vertically integrate
  - Ericsson supplies systems to operators, but is not involved in network operations or distribution of services
  - Motorola is a service provider and network operator for paging and PAMR to date

- Whether or not to internationalize network operation and services distribution
  - Vodafone is aiming at internationalization of network operations and in service provision
- The most profitable approach now may not be the most profitable one in five years.

The main issues regarding vertical integration are:

- Infrastructure and terminal markets will continue to grow rapidly until 1997–1998 then stabilize
  - Stabilization of demand will shrink profit margins and may lead to concentration of supply
- Network operators work with a long payback period (8 to 10 years)
  - Manufacturers' financial structures are not typically the same
- Network operators are not usually set up to manage manufacturing
- Vertical integration
  - Has face value appeal
  - But can it be managed profitably?

The main issues regarding internationalization are:

- Network operators may find it difficult to obtain licenses in foreign nations
- True open markets may be some time in the future.

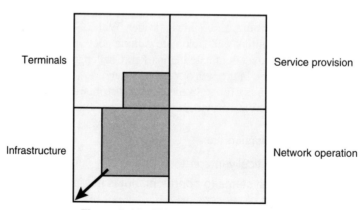

Figure 3.14   Ericsson supply position.

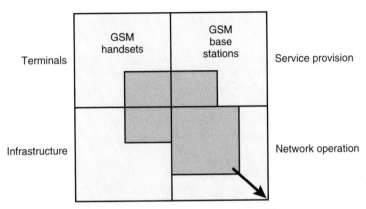

Figure 3.15   Vodaphone supply position.

The key strategic thrusts of three major suppliers are illustrated in Figures 3.14 through 3.16 using a matrix of the four basic components of the supply chain: Infrastructure, network operations, service provision, and terminal supply. Ericsson has a strong position in infrastructure and that is a strategic thrust for the company. Vodafone is strong in network operation and that is a strategic thrust as well. They also provide infrastructure and are active in GSM terminals and base stations. Motorola is active in terminals and infrastructure as well as the other two areas and seems to have strategic thrusts in three of the four areas. This may seem that it is not an integrated corporate strategy perhaps due to the fact that Motorola is run as very autonomous business units, a structure that seems to be serving Motorola very well.

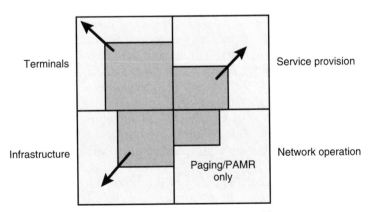

Figure 3.16   Motorola supply position.

Satellite Systems

In the last section of this chapter, we take a look at satellite systems and discuss how they fit in with cellular systems. Satellite systems are capable of huge footprints. They can cover traffic over the oceans and in the air and have been used for these purposes for years. They are also extremely useful for positioning and navigation systems, first for ships and planes, and presently for an increasing number of special applications that rely on knowing the position of the user, for instance, map systems. The spectrum allocated to satellite communications by the International Telecommunications union is

- Mobile transmit: 190–2,010 MHz
- Base transmit: 2,170–2,200 MHz.

The major application of satellite in relation to cellular is to cover remote, sparsely populated areas where putting a cellular infrastructure is not cost-effective. The satellite is, in effect, filling in the holes of coverage of cellular. This allows the world traveler to use cellular wherever it is available, and when in a remote area such an oil exploration field, or a remote mining area, he can use satellite. There are plans of making a combined GSM/Iridium phone, for example. The phone would search for a GSM base station first. If it cannot find one, it defaults to seeking one of the Iridium satellites flying by in a low Earth satellite.

The major types of satellite systems are:

- GEO: Geostationary. 35,786 Km altitude
- LEO: Low Earth Orbit. About 1,000-Km altitude
- MEO: Medium Earth Orbit. About 10,000-Km altitude
- HEO: Highly Elliptical Orbits. Widely variable orbits.

Figure 3.17 plots these systems roughly to scale to put them in perspective. It takes three GEO satellites to cover the earth up to over 70° latitude, that covers most of the populated areas of the earth. The poles are not covered. In contrast, it takes about a dozen MEO satellites flying at about 10,000-Km altitude to cover the same area. For LEOs, the number of satellites is on the order of 60 at a height of about 1,000-Km. HEO satellites are unusual. There are very few systems in operation. Their orbits come very close to the earth and go a great distance.

All satellite systems except for GEO require some fuel to stay in orbit. GEO satellites stay in the same spot relative to the earth by the gravitational pull of the earth combined with that of the moon and the sun. The other satellite systems have a much shorter life, because they run out of fuel. The major public satellite systems in operation or in the planning phases are shown in Figure 3.18.

The GEO systems are established satellite systems that are used for maritime and aeronautical applications. The LEO systems are all in the planning and initial construction stages. Iridium has been planned for some time. It is anticipated that it will provide service by 1998. Initial estimates of the cost of service has dropped from more than $3 per minute to below $2 per minute.

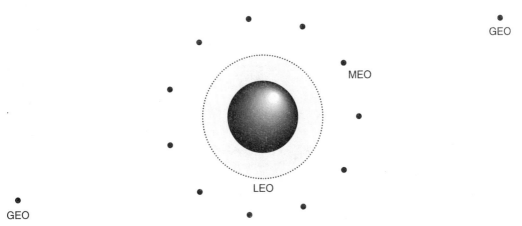

Figure 3.17 Satellite systems in perspective.

This would make it an attractive backup to a global cellular system for the world traveler who needs to stay in contact even when in remote areas that are not covered by cellular.

Globastar is a later entry that has created competition for Iridium. It uses CDMA technology and has fewer satellites than Iridium at a higher altitude.

Teledesic is in the initial planning stages. It is extremely ambitious. It is unlike the others in that it is not for direct connection to a mobile phone. Rather, it is a backbone network that has the intent of providing wide bandwidth service to all areas of the world. It is a trunking system that would connect every remote village in the world. The connection would terminate at a small phone switch in the remote area and provide service to the community. Services such as education, news, and entertainment, as well as many other yet undefined types of information would be communicated. In essence, Teledesic has the vision of being a worldwide, totally ubiquitous, high bandwidth communications network.

Figure 3.18 Public satellite systems.

It was started by an initial investment of $5 million by Bill Gates of Microsoft, and $5 million from Craig McCaw formerly of McCaw Cellular. With this seed money, the company is in search of in excess of $100 billion to construct the system. Each satellite will have an ATM switch on board, and all the satellites will be interconnected with each other as well as with the Public Switched Network, of course. Initial reaction to this idea has ranged from humor to total disbelief. A deeper look reveals a glimmer of possibility. The company plans on using space pebble technology from the Space Defense Initiative research that was done in the past. They have ideas of launching the large number of satellites and replenishing them using mass production methods and multiple vehicle launch techniques. If any two people can do something that ambitious, we could not ask for two more adventurous people. We can look forward to at least a valiant effort that may change the world of communications around the earth forever!

The major differences between GEOs and LEOs are:

- Global coverage up to 75° with 3 satellites
  - 250 ms delay
  - High power needed
- LEO
  - Low power
  - Low delay
  - Many satellites
  - Short life
  - Rapid movement.

A portable GEO phone fills a large briefcase, costs more than $10,000, and more than $5 per minute to operate. To have a small portable phone similar to cellular, we most likely have to use low earth orbit designs. There are some efforts underway to make a GEO system with small lightweight handsets but it has not been introduced as yet.

Summary

In this chapter, we presented the major cellular systems in the world, compared them to each other, and to satellite systems. We started with analog cellular systems including AMPS, NMT, and TACS. Then we discussed the three competing digital cellular standards, namely GSM/DCS, TDMA, and CDMA. The race is on. GSM has an early lead. Whoever maintains an early lead may be the eventual big winner because whoever reaches large volumes first can reduce cost first and expand market share even more. The advanced technology of CDMA is working both for and against the system. Its complexity is proving a difficult hurdle to overcome in the early implementations, but that very complexity is what may make it a winner in the long term as it has the potential of providing the most efficient system for future high density applications.

4 GSM/DCS

GSM/DCS 1800 is an important international standard, as it is the leading digital cellular standard being implemented throughout the world. Its first appearance in the United States is in the form of DCS 1900, one of the PCS standards we will discuss in a later chapter. In this chapter we discuss the capabilities and inner workings of GSM/DCS 1800. In particular:

- GSM objectives
- GSM services
  - Voice services
  - Short message services
  - Data services
  - Fax services
  - Supplementary services
  - Subscriber Identity Module (SIM)
  - Security functions
- GSM Functional architecture
  - Operation and maintenance management
  - Call management
  - Mobility management
  - Radio resources management
- GSM Signaling systems
  - Establishing and releasing calls
  - Call progress indication
  - Handover management
  - Special feature management
  - Short message transmission

- GSM technology
  - Speech coding
  - Modulation scheme
  - Frame format
  - Cellularization
- GSM security operation
  - Authentication process
  - Information privacy.

Service Objectives of GSM/DCS

The primary service objectives of GSM/DCS as stated in the standard are:

- Mobility of users
- Voice services
- Data services
- Vehicle mounted as well as hand-held.

Additional objectives are stated as follows:

- Voice quality as good as first generation cellular
- Encryption of information without great cost penalty
- High spectrum efficiency
- Utilization of the band of 890–915, 935–960 MHz
- Following relevant CCITT recommendations for interconnection of existing switching centers
- Allowing different charging structures for different networks.

The voice quality objective is not to match wire line voice quality. To allow bandwidth conservation, the less stringent objective above was specified. Encryption is important as long as it does not unduly burden the system. The last objective allows users to roam among different service providers.

The GSM/DCS standard was developed over a period of about 10 years for Phase 1. It is well-thought through and has many "neat" features that go beyond the basic requirements. Some of those "neat" features include:

- Power control
  - To reduce interference energy
  - To save battery life

- Discontinuous transmission
  - Turns off transmitter when user is silent
  - Saves battery life
  - Reduces interference energy
- Mobile assisted handover measurements about neighboring cells
- Frequency hopping to combat fading.

Power control is one of the capabilities of CDMA that allows it to claim such high band-width efficiency. The power control in GSM does not create additional channels explicitly. However it does improve the service quality. At a future date, perhaps, it will yield additional channels if some form of dynamic channel allocation mechanism is developed.

Discontinuous transmission is an excellent idea and can save a significant amount of battery life, since most speakers are silent almost half of the time, thus in a full duplex channel, the utilization may be as low as 30 percent. Frequency hopping is implemented at the option of the service provider. It is used to ease the problem of fading. Most service providers have not found it to be necessary.

One of the core functions of a cellular system is to locate the mobile at any point in time. There are three options:

- Page to a single cell
- Page to the whole network
- Page to "location areas."

The first method requires that the mobile update the network every time it changes cells thereby creating much updating traffic. The second method totally eliminates this traffic but creates much paging traffic since the network does not know where the mobile is and must send the page to the whole network. The third method is intermediate. It defines "location areas," which can be, for example, a group of cells served by a single Mobile Switching Center. This is the method used by GSM.

Handover and roaming are defined as follows: Handover is moving through cells and maintaining connection through the cell change; Roaming is being able to move from different service provider networks. This could be to a different country or to a competing service provider in the same area. At this time, no roaming between GSM 900 and DCS 1800 is possible. It can be done if dual mode phones are built.

GSM teleservices are defined as follows:

- Telephony is most important
- Connection between the mobile network and the fixed telephone network including PSTN and ISDN
- Emergency connection to the nearest emergency service by dialing 112
- Group 3 fax using interface at the handset and interface at the telephone network.

The short message service is an innovative feature of GSM. It is essentially advanced two-way paging. Its maximum length is 140 characters. The messages are kept in the network if the receiver is not reachable. Short messaging cell broadcast applications include road condition information. This kind of short message is not encrypted or addressed. It is sent to all users in a given cell. The reason will become obvious when we discuss how it is derived from the signaling structure of GSM.

The GSM bearer services provide both data and fax capabilities. For both services, terminal equipment as well as network equipment are needed. This means that a data device must be installed between the computer or fax machine and the GSM phone, then a signal informs the network that this is a data or a fax call and must connect the appropriate fax modem or data modem at the network end to prepare the signal for transmission on the public network.

GSM supplementary services are similar to those available in the PSTN and include:

- Outgoing call barring
- Call forwarding if unreachable or if busy
- Calling party identification
- Conferencing
- Closed user groups.

Call forwarding is used often with mobile phones and usually leads to a voice mail system that is offered as part of the service. When a voice message is left for a user, a short message is sent to the user to inform him that he has a message. Some service providers store faxes as well and inform the user via a short message that he has a fax waiting. The user can then call and have the fax delivered to his notebook computer, to a fax machine in the hotel where he is staying, or to a remote office where he is working.

Closed user groups are essentially virtual private networks. They provide special billing for calls within the group. Moreover, they can restrict calling to within the group if desired for outgoing calls, incoming calls, or both. This is an important feature especially in the future when we may need to share infrastructure between public and private applications.

The Subscriber Identity Module is an innovative idea that has more applications than were originally conceived. It contains all the subscribe specific data including:

- User's phone number
- Personal private key
- Preferred network
- Charging information
- Abbreviated dialing list
- Store of short messages.

It is the size of a credit card or postage stamp. Every GSM phone has one that can be removed. It allows a user to put it into any phone that is designed to the GSM SIM interface specification and have

Modem type	Data rate	Async	Synch
V.21	300 bps	*	
V.22	1,200 bps	*	*
V.22 bis	2,400 bps		*
V.23	1,200/75 bps	*	
V.26 ter	2,400 bps		*
V.32	4,800, 9,600 bps		*

Figure 4.1 Modem types supported.

that phone become personalized to him. For example, if the user is visiting in some area that uses a different system with a different air interface, the user can rent a phone with that air interface, plug in his SIM, and have his personal information in that phone. This is the concept of SIM roaming.

The security functions of GSM are three-fold:

- The SIM is authenticated before access to the network is allowed
- Voice and data traffic is encrypted
- The user location is protected in the network.

To combat cellular fraud, the authentication process ensures that user keys are never transmitted in the clear. This is discussed in detail later in this chapter. Encryption of the voice and data traffic insures privacy. The location of the cell in which the user is located at any point in time is also kept private except from law enforcement agencies or other government agencies. Security can be turned on or off by the service providers. Some providers have elected to implement a weaker form of the security, or not to implement it at all. Some governments have complained that the encryption process is too good, thus preventing them from being able to listen in for national security purposes.

The modem types supported by GSM are shown in Figure 4.1.

Functional Architecture

The functional architecture of GSM are shown if Figure 4.2. As mentioned before, every GSM phone has a SIM card. The SIM interface is a standard that can be used by any cellular system. If it is used, it allows anyone with a SIM card to roam to that system and carry along his iden-

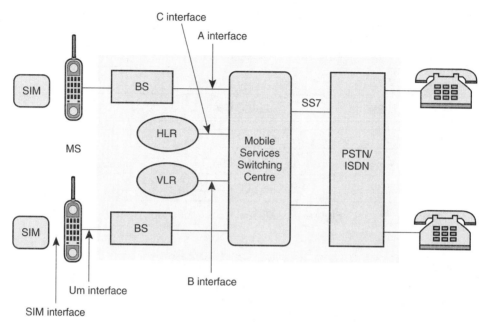

Figure 4.2   GSM Functional architecture.

tity. The air interface is in the Um interface. Terminal manufacturers build the phones to that inter-face. The phones speak on that interface to the base stations. The box marked BS in the figure is composed of the Base Station Transceiver (BST) as well as the Base Station Controller (BSC). The base stations are built to speak the Um interface to the phones and the A interface to the Mobile Switching Center (MSC). The MSC then speaks SS7 to the public-switched network.

The Home Location Registers are where all the user information is stored including their phone numbers, the services they subscribe to, their secret keys, and other information. The collec-tion of HLRs in a country, or indeed throughout the world, can be regarded as a giant distributed database of all the mobile users worldwide. This information is accessed by the SS7 packet-switched network whenever someone makes a call to a mobile user. The call must first be directed to the HLR of the called user. That is where his whereabouts are known. When the user is roaming in another part of the network, the HLR provides the locations of the VLR that is serving the user at that point in time. The call is then set up to that location.

The HLRs and VLRs are built to the B and C interface. These interfaces are open not only to allow different manufacturers to build them but also to provide an open interface to future database and information services. This is an important trend. We used to pay a large sum for the phone and for the air time. Now we can obtain the phone for little or nothing, but still pay quite a bit for the air time. In the future, some say we will pay nothing for the phone, a little or nothing for the air time, and pay mostly for the information services we are accessing. The information will reside on servers that are connected to the network via the B and C interfaces.

The frequency allocations for GSM 900 and DCS 1800 are shown in Figure 4.3. GSM 900 has 50 MHz total at 900 MHz. DCS 1800 has three times as much at twice the frequency. The total number of channels using the 13 Kbps vocoding rate is about 1,000 full duplex channels for GSM and 3,000 for DCS.

Many suppliers are looking at DCS as simply a new set of frequencies for meeting growing market demand. The new frequencies require many more cell sites due to the higher frequency and the lower power. Another way to look at DCS is as a high density service for dense applications, whereas GSM is a low density service for applications in less dense areas such as the roadways and areas between large metropolitan areas. The physical and MAC layer of GSM/DCS are:

- Modulation—Gaussian Minimum Shift Keying (GMSK)
- MAC—FDMA/TDMA
- Duplexing—FDD.

The power classes for GSM and DCS are shown in Figure 4.4. The most commonly used power levels are 2 w for the GSM handsets, and 8 w for the vehicle mounted units. The other power levels are not frequently used. DCS has the much lower power levels shown. The GSM channelization scheme is described by:

- 50-MHz total allocation
- 200-KHz carrier spacing
- 124 pairs of FDMA super channels
- Each FDMA superchannel has a data rate of 270 Kbps
- Each FDMA superchannel provides 8 TDMA traffic channels
- Voice uses Residually Excited Linear Predictive (RELP) coding running at 13 Kbps
- There is a total of $8 \times 124 = 992$ full duplex channels.

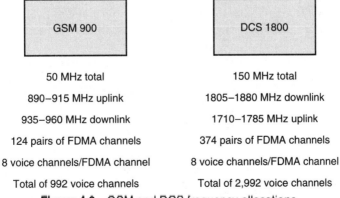

GSM 900	DCS 1800
50 MHz total	150 MHz total
890–915 MHz uplink	1805–1880 MHz downlink
935–960 MHz downlink	1710–1785 MHz uplink
124 pairs of FDMA channels	374 pairs of FDMA channels
8 voice channels/FDMA channel	8 voice channels/FDMA channel
Total of 992 voice channels	Total of 2,992 voice channels

Figure 4.3 GSM and DCS frequency allocations.

Class	GSM 900	DCS 1800
1	20 w	1 w
2	8 w	0.25 w
3	5 w	
4	2 w	
5	0.8 w	

Figure 4.4   GSM and DCS power levels.

Multiplying the rate per voice channel, 13 Kbps by the number of channels per carrier, 8 yields 104 Kbps, yet the data rate of the carrier is more than twice that at 270 Kbps. Where do all the extra bits go? We will see the answer to that when we discuss the signaling and error handling schemes of GSM. This kind of level of overhead is common in cellular networks. The DCS channelization scheme is described by:

- 150-MHz total allocation
- 200-KHz carrier spacing
- 374 pairs of FDMA superchannels
- Each FDMA superchannel has a data rate of 270 Kbps
- Each FDMA superchannel provides 8 TDMA traffic channels
- Voice uses Residually Excited Linear Predictive (RELP) coding running at 13 Kbps
- There is a total of $8 \times 374 = 2,992$ full duplex channels.

The DCS 1800 channelization is almost exactly three times that of GSM 900, just a bit more than three times. Three times 124 superchannels is 372. Instead, DCS 1800 obtains two extra pairs of superchannels.

The raw data rate of a voice grade channel is 13 Kbps. The typical data rates that are provided to the end user are:

- 9.6 Kbps
- 4.8 Kbps
- 2.4 Kbps.

This limitation stems from the scheme of allocating a single voice grade channel to data traffic. As the demand for higher bandwidth channels matures, this limitation will have to be overcome. Some proposals are already being made for GSM Phase 2+. The proposals involve aggregating multiple voice channels to provide greater throughput. This kind of method is used by DECT to obtain data bearer services on the order of 0.5 Mbps. This is possible with DECT, because its carrier runs at a very high rate on the order of 1 Mbps. For GSM, the FDMA superchannel carrier runs at 270 Kbps. Hence, we can expect this kind of voice channel combining scheme will be able to yield total throughput maximums on the order of 100 Kbps. Still this is a very nice rate for wide area networking, and will open the door for many exciting new applications. This kind of plan is called Wide Band Circuit Switched (WBCS) data.

The voice and data services of GSM and DCS are provided as follows:

- Voice channel—One traffic channel
- Data channel—One traffic channel
- Future wide band data—Multiple traffic channels up to eight
- Short message service—Signaling channel that equals 1/8 of a traffic channel
- Short message cell broadcast service—Cell broadcast channel used for paging receivers that equal 1/16 of a traffic channel.

The definitions of traffic channels are given by:

- TCH/F: Traffic channel, full rate
  - 13 Kbps
  - One full-rate voice channel
  - One data channel at 9.6, 4.8, or 2.4 Kbps
- TCH/H: Traffic channel, half rate
  - 7 Kbps
  - One half-rate voice channel
  - One data channel at 4.8, or 2.4 Kbps.

A traffic channel full rate provides the basic voice channel, or a full data channel. The half channel is defined with half-rate codecs in mind and can provide data at the lower rates.

GSM/DCS Signaling

The purposes of signaling are to establish and release calls, to give call progress indication, to do handover management, and to provide special features such as call forwarding and short message service. There are two types of signaling channels in GSM/DCS:

- Signaling associated with a call
- Signaling outside a call.

The signaling associated with a call has two subtypes:

- Slow Associated Control Channel: SACCH
- Fast Associated Control Channel: FACCH.

The SACCH is used mainly for sending radio measurements for handover decisions. It is also used for other nonurgent procedures. About two messages per second can be sent in each direction. The transmission delay is on the order of a half a second. The FACCH is used for call establishment, authentication of the SIM, handover commands, and other high urgency messages. The FACCH uses the traffic channel itself before the call is set up and after it is completed. While the call is in progress, the FACCH "steals" bits from the voice or data traffic to perform functions such as handover commands. For voice, this stealing is not noticeable; for data it is handled by the error protocol in the cellular modem, or data set.

There are many other signals that are used to make GSM work. These other signals are outside the call and use other channels for that purpose. This is where all the extra bits in the overall data rate of 270 Kbps go. The signals that are outside the call are summarized as follows:

- The base station sends synchronization bursts periodically to the mobiles to
  - Perform frame synchronization
  - Fine-tune the frequency
- The base station sends its ID and parameters periodically on a
  - Broadcast Control Channel: BCCH
- Authentication and other call setup signals are sent on a
  - Stand-alone Dedicated Control Channel: SDCCH
- A request for a channel by a mobile is sent on a
  - Random Access Channel: RACH
- An access grant of a channel is sent to a mobile on a
  - Access Grant Channel
- The system initiates a call to a mobile on a
  - Paging Channel: PCH.

The Stand-alone Dedicated Control Channel (SDCCH) is sometimes referred to as a TCH/8, because it is equivalent to 1/8 of a Traffic Channel (TCH). It is used for authentication and special feature management, and it is the channel from which the Short Message Service is derived.

The mobile can be in one of three modes. It can be turned off or it can be in the idle mode, where it is turned on, but the user is not talking on it or sending data or a fax through it. In the idle mode, the mobile is performing several functions in order to stay in synchronization with the base station, and to handle handovers that may occur. It is listening for paging messages that would alert it of an incoming call. It is monitoring signal quality and sending that information to the base station as an input to handover. In addition, it is receiving the Cell Broadcast Short Messages. The third mode is the dedicated mode where a mobile station has a Traffic Channel (TCH) dedicated to it and the user is actively on that channel.

Access to the network is handled on the above and some additional signaling channels as follows:

- Mobile achieves and maintains synchronization with the base station using
  - Synchronization channel: SCH
  - Frequency Correction Channel: FCCH
- The base station sends general information to the mobile on
  - Broadcast Control Channel: BCCH
- Mobile sends a request for a channel on
  - Random Access Channel: RACH
- Base station responds on
  - Paging and Access Grant Channel: PAGCH.

The Cell Broadcast Short Message is an 80-octet message that can be sent every two seconds. It uses half of TCH/8. It relies on the Cell Broadcast Channel (CBCH).

GSM/DCS Frequency/Time Plan

A channel in GSM is a time slot repeated every frame on one frequency for one direction, and on another time slot repeated every frame on another frequency for the other direction. This channel scheme is depicted in Figure 4.5. The base station transmits on the downlink higher frequencies. The mobile transmits on the uplink lower frequency. There are eight time slots per FDMA
superchannel. The downlink is time shifted from the uplink to give the mobile and base time to shift from transmit to receive. This general plan is the most common for digital cellular systems. The frame format for each FDMA superchannel is shown if Figure 4.6. The most common kind of frame, or burst is a normal burst. This is the kind of burst that is used for traffic channels. On every burst there are Tail bits and a Guard period. The Guard period is to allow for errors in clock synchronization accuracy, and differing distances of the mobiles from the base station, which are minimized by Time advance as will be discussed shortly. The training sequence is used to maintain synchronization and is inserted in the middle of the frame to give it the best average effect on the whole frame. In a synchronization burst, the training sequence occupies the largest section of the frame. The Access burst is the kind of frame used for mobiles to request a channel. The request is made at random during the extra long Guard period. If the mobile encounters a collision with another mobile requesting a channel, it waits a random time and tries again. This kind of operation is similar to a Local Area Network protocol.

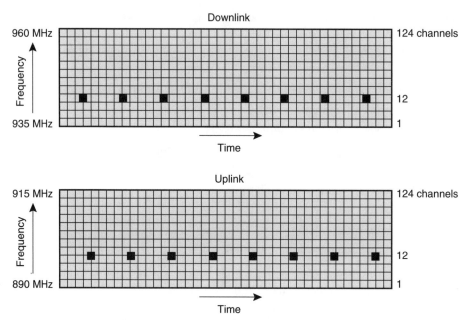

Figure 4.5   GSM/DCS frequency/time slots.

Logically, every Traffic Channel (TCH) is permanently associated with a SACCH for nonurgent messages such as sending transmission information. For urgent messages a FAACH is used before and after the call, and during the call by stealing. These and other signaling channels are mapped onto the frame hierarchy that are depicted in Figure 4.7. The basic frame that we discussed in Figure 4.6 is at the bottom of Figure 4.7. The structure above is logical and serves as the basis of organization and for setting timers for cycling certain functions such as slow frequency hopping and setting frame numbering for security and other purposes. The multiframes are multiples of the basic frame. There are two kinds of multiframe. The 51 multiframes are more appropriate for signaling frames. The 26 multiframes are more appropriate for traffic channels. Superframes are the smallest multiple of both the 51 signaling frames and the 26 traffic frames. The hyperframe serves as the basis for frame numbering. It is about 3½ hours long. It is the smallest cycle for frequency hopping and encryption.

Error detection and correction is provided to protect against external and internal interference. In most cellular systems such as GSM, internal interference is greater than external interference. The internal interference comes from other users in neighboring cells using the same channel sets. There are three types of error detection and correction codes used in GSM:

- Parity codes for error detection
- Cyclic codes for bursty error detection and correction
- Block convolutional codes for error correction (Viterbi Codes)

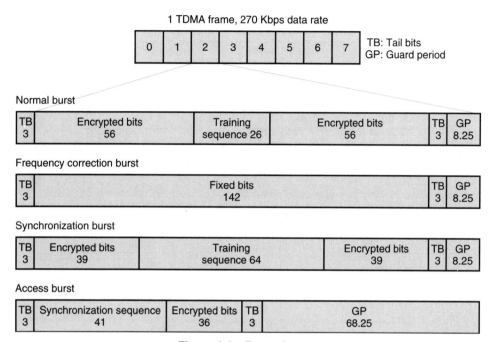

Figure 4.6 Frame format.

This is another place where all the extra bits in the 270-Kbps frame go. The alternative is not to do as much error detection and correction, and to rely more on retransmission to take care of errors. It is a trade-off, and for cellular, the trade-off leans toward more error detection and correction than for cordless and PCS systems. The block convolutional codes are Viterbi codes, named after Andrew Viterbi who is one of the primary forces behind the CDMA digital cellular standard.

There are three-link layer protocols that are used to exchange signaling information between different entities in the GSM architecture, for example, BST, BSC, HLR, VLR, and the SS7 network. The three-link layer protocols are :

- Link Access Control for Mobile D channel (LAPDm) for the air interface from the mobile to the base station
- LAPD on the A-bis interface from the base station to the switching center
- Message Transfer Protocol (MTP) to the SS7 network and to the HLRs and VLRs.

This is illustrated in Figure 4.8.

Radio resource management is a layer 3 set of protocols. When a mobile is first put into service it scans the network to find a synchronization channel. If it finds one, it synchronizes to it and goes into the idle mode waiting for:

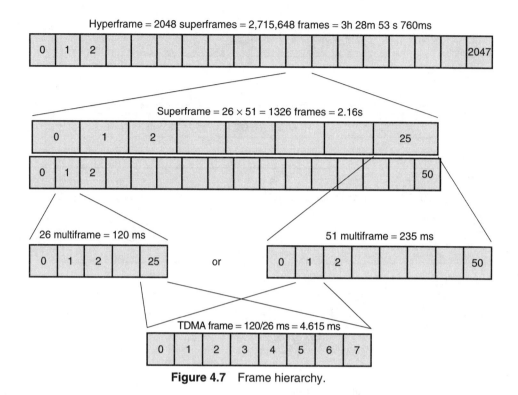

Figure 4.7   Frame hierarchy.

- A page indicating an incoming call
- The user to press the send button that initiated a request for a channel from the network.

The paging channels are slotted at specific times. This allows the mobile to spend most of the time of the idle mode asleep to conserve battery power. It wakes up during the slotted paging channel to see if there is a call for it. If there is not, it goes back to sleep till the next slotted paging channel.

The power is adjusted to the minimum required both at the base station as well as at the mobile. This not only conserves battery power at the mobile, but it also limits the internal interference generated by the system, and ultimately can increase the number of channels available in GSM. As mentioned previously, this increase is not taken into account explicitly. The power is adjusted every 60 ms over a range of 26 dB, for example, from 20 mw to 8 w.

To reduce the size of the required Guard periods, a Time advance is inserted by the mobiles who are the edge of the cell. The maximum size of a cell in GSM is 35 Km. This produces a round trip delay of 233 µs. The mobile at the edge of the cell advances its transmission by a time that it calculates based on information it receives from the base station. The base station monitors the

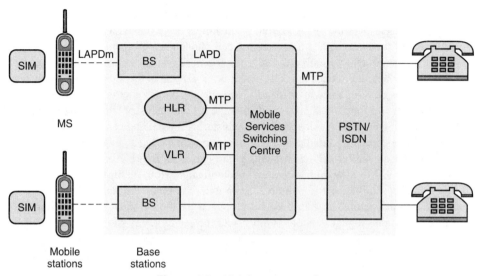

Figure 4.8 Link layer protocols.

value of the Time advance and uses it as an input for the decision to make a handover. The longer the Time advance, the more likely the base station is to order a cell change.

Handover is performed by the BSC based on information gathered by the base station and by the mobile. The handover decision is made based on four factors:

- Error rate
- Transmitter power
- Received signal strength
- Time advance.

All these factors are indicators that the mobile is at the edge of the cell and would benefit from a cell change. The algorithm for combining these factors is left up to the service provider.

GSM/DCS Security

Security has three parts:
- Authentication
- Data privacy
- Privacy of user location.

Authentication is important in preventing cellular fraud. With analog cellular, the mobiles transmit their identity in the clear over the air. An intruder can simple drive down the street and collect these identities. Later, they enter these identities into the cell phone and sell them. The buyers can make calls anywhere they wish, and the calls are charged to the valid owner of that identity. When the user receives his monthly bill and notices the calls he did not make, he notifies the cellular provider who apologizes and issues the user a new user identity. Meanwhile, the intruder is driving down the street again collecting new user identifications. Fraud costs the cellular industry billions of dollars. In addition, it causes users a great inconvenience. They are disturbed by the huge erroneous bills; they have to contact the cellular company, and then they have to deal with having a new phone number.

Authentication in digital cellular systems greatly reduces fraud. Authentication in GSM is depicted in Figure 4.9. After the mobile requests authentication from the BSC, the BSC generates a random number and sends it to the mobile. The mobile combines the random number with the user's secret key that is stored in the SIM and protected by the Personal Identification Number. The algorithm for combining the random number with the secret key is known as the A3 ciphering algorithm. The result is sent to the BSC. The BSC performs a similar operation. It has the user's secret key stored in the HLR. It uses the A3 ciphering algorithm and obtains the result. It compares the result with that obtained from the mobile. It they are the same, it grants access to the mobile.

Note that the only information that goes over the air is the random number and the result. The A3 ciphering algorithm is designed so that if those quantities are known, it is extremely difficult to decipher the secret key.

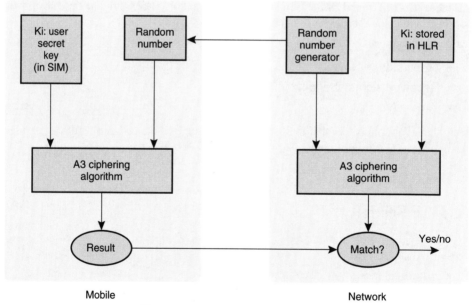

Figure 4.9 Authentication process.

With such an authentication process, an intruder can drive down the street collecting random numbers and results all day, and he will not be able to decipher user secret keys unless they have access to a huge computer and endless processing time. There is still the possibility that the defrauder can sign up with the cellular company and obtain service, make as many calls as possible, and then disappear without paying the bill, but this not a technical problem. This can be done with any system and can be minimized by better credit checks and user qualification before offering them service.

The data privacy process is shown in Figure 4.10. The process starts the same way as for authentication. The BSC sends the mobile a random number. The mobile uses a second ciphering algorithm, A8, to combine the random number with its secret key. The result is a connection key. This connection key is combined with the frame number using a third ciphering algorithm. The result is combined with the data through an exclusive OR. This means that the connection key is different for every frame of data. Recall that the frame numbers start over only every hyperframe. This means that every frame has a different connection key for messages lasting all the way up to about 3½ hours.

This data privacy scheme is very strong. In fact, some governments have complained that it is too strong and prevents them from monitoring cellular traffic for national security reasons. Some countries choose not to implement data privacy. Some countries choose to implement a less complex system.

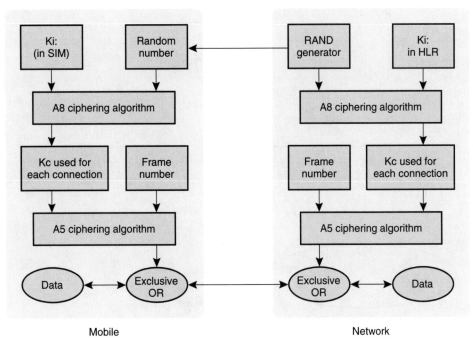

Figure 4.10   Encryption process

The last part of security is the privacy of the user location. The knowledge of which cell the user is in resides in the network. This knowledge is kept private except possibly from government agencies. This is akin to the phone company allowing police departments to trace calls in the wired network to help locate illegal activities.

Mobility Handling

Each cellular operator's network is called a Public Land Mobile Network (PLMN). Hence, in moving from one country to another, or from one part of a country to another, the user encounters different PLMNs. In addition, with competition, the user can encounter multiple PLMNs in the same area.

A mobile is identified by its International Mobile Subscriber Identity. The IMSI contains:

- The user's personal phone number
- The number of the PLMN that offers him primary service
- His country code.

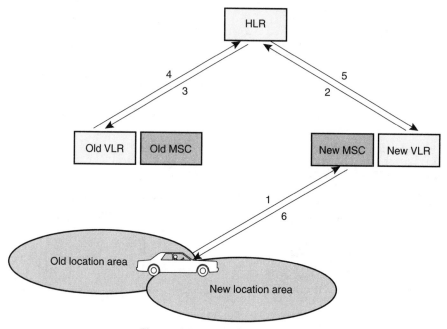

Figure 4.11   Location updating.

The mobile sends its IMSI whenever it changes "location areas." Recall that "location areas" are collections of base stations that are served by an MSC. The IMSIs are stored in the VLR serving this MSC. This event is reported by the VLR to the user's HLR. When someone calls this user, the call initiation goes to the user's HLR. The HLR informs the MSC of the calling party of the whereabouts of the user; it tells it which MSC the user is served by at the moment. The network then sets up the call from the calling party to the user at the serving MSC.

Figure 4.11 depicts what happens when the user changes location areas. When the mobile moves from the area served by the old MSC, it registers with the new MSC. The new VLR inputs the user's data into its database, and informs the user's HLR of the event. The HLR informs the old VLR of the event, and the user now belongs to the new MSC and new VLR.

Summary

In this chapter, we began with the objectives of GSM/DCS as stated in the standard. We presented the voice and data features of the system. The voice is based on a 13-Kbps vocoding technique called RELP. Data can be sent up to 9.6 Kbps in Phase 2 of GSM. There are proposals to extend that up to the range of 100 Kbps by combining voice grade channels up to the capacity of one whole carrier. This is a proposal for GSM Phase 2+. Data require data sets to be inserted between the data device and the cellular phone, and a modem or data device to be inserted at the network between the cellular connection and the PSTN.

We presented the functional architecture and discussed the open interfaces that allow different manufacturers to implement different parts of the system, for example, phones, base stations, switching centers, and databases. In particular we pointed out that the SIM interface will see more applications than it was originally envisioned to have.

We discussed the signaling structure of GSM and showed how the system works, and how certain features are obtained: specifically, the Short Message feature and the Cell Broadcast feature. We presented the frequency and time channelization scheme. We detailed the three parts of security of GSM including the authentication process, the data privacy process, and the privacy of the user location. Finally, we showed how mobility is handled as the user moves from one location area served by one MSC to another location area served by another MSC. Next, we will discuss Cordless systems and PCS.

5 *Cordless Telephony and PCS*

Aimed at lower-cost applications and smaller areas of coverage, cordless telephony will be a complement to digital cellular and provide higher density islands of coverage. Early cordless telephony systems will grow into future PCS systems. In this chapter, we discuss:

- Cordless Telephony technologies
  - CT-2 and variations
  - DECT
  - Wireless PBXs
  - Personal Handyphone in Japan
- Personal Communications Systems in the United States
  - Frequency allocations
  - The seven standards being considered
- Comparison of cordless/PCS and cellular
- Future third-generation cellular systems including UMTS and FPLMTS.

Now, we will focus on the cordless cluster in Figure 5.1 reproduced here for convenience. This cluster has smaller cell sizes and provides higher data rate, particularly in the case of DECT.

Analog Cordless

First, we start with the roots of cordless, analog cordless. Figure 5.2 summarizes the situation. In the United States, in 1995, there were 60 million analog cordless phones in people's homes. The total population of the United States is about 250 million people. The average number of people per home is around three or four. That means that there is a cordless phone in almost

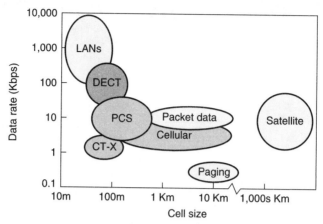

Figure 5.1   Network positioning.

every home in the United States! This is phenomenal growth considering the fairly poor quality of these phones. There is no standard for cordless phones in the United States. The range of the sets is very short; it barely covers a large house. Voice quality is acceptable at best. Security is often nonexistent. One can walk down the street and pick up dial tone, or worse, ongoing conversations from neighboring houses. Yet people buy them freely. This shows the desirability of being free of the cord. And this is why suppliers are so excited about future PCS systems. People will buy them in large numbers if the price is right.

The number of cordless phones in the United States is growing at 15 million per year. They operate in the 50-MHz band, and cost somewhere between $50 and $100. There is a model that runs in the ISM band at 900 MHz that costs about $250 and provides much greater range than the lower-cost models. They can reach as far as one mile. So one can take them to the neighbor's house, or down the street, but not very far away from the base station.

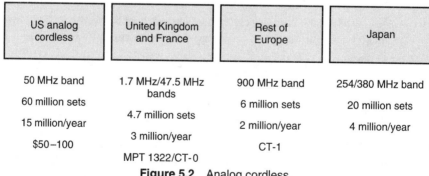

US analog cordless	United Kingdom and France	Rest of Europe	Japan
50 MHz band	1.7 MHz/47.5 MHz bands	900 MHz band	254/380 MHz band
60 million sets		6 million sets	20 million sets
15 million/year	4.7 million sets	2 million/year	4 million/year
$50–100	3 million/year	CT-1	
	MPT 1322/CT-0		

Figure 5.2   Analog cordless.

Japan is the other part of the world where cordless phones are prevalent. They had 20 million sets in 1995 growing at a rate of 4 million per year. They operate in the higher band of 254 to 380 MHz. In Europe, there are not as many cordless phones. The United Kingdom and France had about 5 million sets in 1995 growing at 3 million per year. There they do have a standard; it is MPT 1322, which is sometimes called CT-0. The rest of Europe had 6 million sets in 1995 growing at a rate of 2 million per year. The standard used there is CT-1.

Analog cordless in the United States has the following parameters:

- 46.6–47.0 MHz = 400 KHz, base station transmit
- 49.6–50.0 MHz = 400 KHz, handset transmit
- 10 frequency pairs, separated by 40 KHz
- Signal bandwidth of 20 KHz
- 20 uw Effective Radiated Power
- Analog FM voice
- Digital signaling
- 15 more frequency bands are planned in the 44 MHz and the 49 MHz bands.

The frequency is much lower than cellular systems. The transmitted power is extremely low, and hence the very short range. The analog FM voice modulation and digital signaling is similar to analog cellular. The extreme popularity has prompted the FCC to more than double the allocation.

In the United Kingdom, the CT-0 standard was developed. It provides eight channel pairs. The base unit transmits in the 1.7 MHz band, extremely low. The handset transmits in the 47.5 MHz band. France is also adopting this standard. In the rest of Europe, in response to high demand, CEPT developed CT-1. This standard has the following parameters:

- 914–915 = 1 MHz, handset transmits
- 959–960 = 1 MHz, base transmits
- 40 channel pairs, separated by 25 KHz
- An additional 80 channel pairs are planned in the future
  - 885–887 = 2 MHz, handset transmits
  - 930–932 = 2 MHz, base transmits.

CT-1 is a coexistence standard, not an interoperability standard. This means that different models will not interfere with each other. They can coexist, but they cannot interoperability, so a base station from one supplier cannot work with a handset from another vendor. This is not much of an issue for a residential cordless system that is composed of one base station and one of a few handsets. A coexistence standard is produced by CEPT. If an interoperability standard were in order, CEPT would have delegated the work to ETSI where more involved standards are developed. We will discuss the standard development process in a later chapter.

In Japan, the parameters of cordless are given by:

- 254 MHz, handset transmits
- 380 MHz, base transmits
- 89 channel pairs
- 12.5 KHz channel spacing
- Analog FM modulation for voice
- 10 mw transmitted power.

Japan had the greatest number of channel pairs initially and higher power relatively speaking.

Digital Cordless

Now, let us turn to digital cordless. Figure 5.3 summarizes the situation. The first digital cordless system to be introduced is CT-2. It was introduced first in Europe. Europe is ahead of the rest of the world in digital cordless systems followed by Asia, and then by North America. The first implementation of CT-2 was for telepoint service. Telepoint service is like a cordless pay phone. It is usually located in shopping centers or other densely populated areas such as airports, or downtown areas. As long as the user is in the vicinity of a base station, he can originate a call. It is oneway outgoing only. Putting in a oneway CT-2 system is very simple compared to putting in a twoway system. This is true particularly because the initial systems did not allow handover. If the user moved from the coverage area of the base station, he lost the connection. So, this kind of telepoint is truly like a cordless pay phone.

The systems that were installed in Europe were called Rabbit for the United Kingdom, and Bibop for France. The services did not capture much interest. It seems that the public took them as seriously as their names implied. In Asia, the services caught on much better, especially when

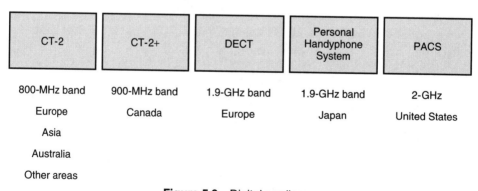

Figure 5.3   Digital cordless.

combined with one-way paging. The combination works as follows. If John wants to call Mary, he pages Mary. If Mary would like to reply, she calls John back on her CT-2 phone. Some manufacturers combined the pager and the CT-2 phone into one set. When Mary receives the page and wants to reply, she simply pushes one button. Since the phone stores the number that John sent to Mary when he paged her, it can dial him back.

Some systems took this one step further. When John pages Mary, he is parked in the network while he holds on the line. While Mary receives the page and decides whether to return the page or not, John receives a ringing signal. If Mary decides to return the call, they are connected. As far as John is concerned, it seems like a two-way phone system. As far as Mary is concerned, it is like a two-way phone system with calling-party number identification. In a way, this ingenious combination is better than a two-way system, because it has calling-party identification.

CT-2 systems have been installed in Hong Kong, China, Malaysia, Singapore, Thailand, and other countries. Even as these systems are being installed, others are losing popularity and will be replaced by high-density cellular systems or PCS systems. In retrospect, CT-2 seems to be serving as an excellent learning tool for more mature systems.

The CT-2 technology is summarized by:

- 864–868 MHz = 4 MHz band (in Europe)
- 40 channels
- 100 KHz spacing
- GFSK modulation
- FDMA, single channel per carrier
- 72 Kbps data rate supporting
  - Two-way voice
  - Signaling
- TDD (Time Division Duplexing)
- 32 Kbps ADPCM voice coding.

The first major difference between this cordless system and the cellular systems we discussed before is that it uses one single frequency band instead of two, one for the uplink, and one for downlink. The reason for this is that the duplexing method is TDD, which is sometimes called ping pong. The reason for this is that the voice goes in one direction in the first part of the frame, then in the other direction in the second part of the frame. The frame is very short, on the order of 2 ms for CT-2, so it is totally unnoticeable for the voice traffic.

Next, we notice that the power is comparatively low, 10 milliwatts instead of 1 watt or more. The voice-coding technique is ADPCM running at 32 Kbps. This is the same voice coding as is used in the wired network, so we should expect voice quality on par with the wired network. What about spectrum efficiency? Cordless systems have small cells, so the frequencies can be reused more often. Moreover, they are optimized for cost, and it is much less expensive to implement ADPCM than it is to implement a sophisticated predictive technique like RELP.

The frequency/time plan for CT-2 is illustrated in Figure 5.4. We can see the ping pong duplexing method used in each carrier. We can also see that there is just one band of frequencies allocated, and that it is divided by straight FDMA. CT-2 is truly a first generation system.

The CT-2 standard itself does support two-way as well as handover. It is just that the early implementations did not implement those capabilities. In Canada, those capabilities were implemented, and they added further enhancement to create CT-2+. CT-2+ is the basis for PCS in Canada. The spectrum allocation for CT-2+ in Canada is 944–948 = 24 MHz, with 948–952 = 4 MHz reserved for future use.

The reason initial CT-2 systems did not implement the two-way and handoff is to make the systems simple. Much of the work on the network side of a cordless or cellular system is involved in locating the user and delivering a call to him. The other large task is to handle handoff from one cell to another as the user moves. In some respects these capabilities require more work than implementing the base stations and the air interface. An analogy is an iceberg. Most of the mass of the iceberg, almost 85 percent of it is under the water. In the same way, a large part of the work of implementing a cellular or two-cordless network is hidden from the user in the network and involves the distributed databases for keeping track of his location, and the signaling systems required to handle the handoff and other mobility functions.

Ericsson proposed CT-3 some time ago as a cordless PBX standard. This standard developed into DECT, which applies not only to wireless PBXs, but also to residential cordless, telepoint service, and wireless loops. The system in Japan is called Personal Handyphone. PACS, or Personal Access Communications System is one of the low-tier standard for PCS in the United States. It is a combination of PHS and a PCS system that was proposed by Bellcore. It is included here, because it is similar to the other cordless systems. It will be discussed in more detail in the PCS section below. Now on to specific details on each of these systems.

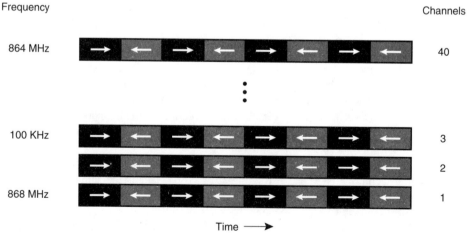

Figure 5.4 CT-2 frequency/time plan.

DECT: Digital European Cordless Telephone

DECT operates in the 1.9 GHz band. The objectives of DECT are to be cost-effective and to provide high-user densities. The technology of DECT can be summarized as follows:

- 1.88–1.90 GHz = 20 MHz
- 10 carriers
- Carriers spaced by 1.728 MHz
- Carrier data rate of 1.152 Mbps
- FDMA/TDMA/TDD
- 12 TDD channels per carrier
- 32 Kbps ADPCM for voice
- 10 mw average transmitted power
- Estimated range
  - 500 meters in free space
  - 50 to 100 meters in typical office environments.

The frequency band for DECT is right above DCS 1800, and right below 2 GHz. It has one of the largest carriers of the systems we have discussed. The reason for that will become apparent when we discuss its data capabilities shortly. It uses TDD for the duplexing method. The average power is low. The range is consistent with indoor use. The large difference in range from free space to office environments is typical. Indoor environments have walls and other obstructions that greatly reduce the range.

The DECT frequency plan is shown in Figure 5.5. The 10 carriers are spaced by 1.72 MHz and have a data rate of 1.152 Mbps, indicating that the channel filters do not need to be extremely sharp, another way of making the overall system inexpensive. The frame format for the 1.152 Mbps carrier is shown in Figure 5.6.

The TDD arrangement is a little different from CT-2. For DECT, the 12 channels all go in one direction, then all come back in the reverse direction. Each slot has 32 bits for synchronization, followed by 64 bits for signaling. The 320 bits for voice or data are repeated every 10 ms, resulting

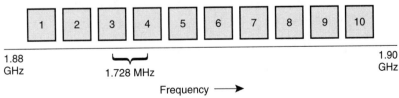

Figure 5.5 DECT frequency plan.

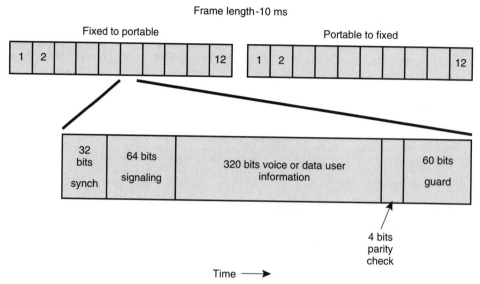

Figure 5.6 DECT frame format.

in a throughput rate of 32 Kbps. A simple parity check comes next for error detection. Finally, there is a 60-bit guard band.

DECT uses dynamic channel allocation. Handsets scan the network for stronger base stations. When they find one, they set up connection on one of the free time slots in the new base station, and request transfer from the base station controller. Dynamic channel allocation decentralizes the handover to the handsets. It is self organizing and has high frequency reuse factor.

The data services of DECT are impressive for a cordless system. The service is provided in Service Data Units or SDUs. The smallest SDU is one voice channel equivalent, or 32 Kbps. More than one voice grade channel can be put together to increase the data rate in increments of 32 Kbps up to the maximum of the whole carrier. If the whole carrier is used, the aggregate data rate is:

- 736 Kbps without error handling
- 588 Kbps with error handling.

This is a very respectable data rate for a cordless telephone system. It rivals data rates of Local Area Networks. In addition, DECT also provides:

- Logically connectionless datagram service
- Support for multicast and broadcast
- Connection time of about 50 ms.

All these are Local Area Networklike services. The one drawback is the connection time. Even though 50 ms is extremely fast for a circuit switch, it is still a bit slow for LAN traffic. The average message on a LAN has a duration on the same order as the connection time. People are used to connection times of about 10 ms, which is what most LANs provide.

DECT also provides virtual circuits, authentication, and data privacy. DECT has a good chance of being a worldwide wireless PBX standard.

Wireless PBXs

In this section, we discuss three wireless PBX technologies. The first one is typical of what most wireless PBXs will look like. The second two are unique implementations that used ingenious techniques to provide early wireless PBX systems before primary spectrum was allocated for that part of the industry.

A wireless PBX system consists of the portable phones, the small base stations, and the base station controller. The controller is connected to the PBX, or a centrex, and essentially provides connectivity to the wired private network. Wireless PBX have many special features including:

- Incoming call screening
- Access to personal and system directories
- Integration with voice mail systems
- System performance monitoring
- Radio performance measurement facilities.

As their wired counterparts, wireless PBXs lead the list of special features. The features of a wireless PBX will far surpass what will be offered on public cellular and PCS systems just as the list of wired PBX features far surpasses the list of features available on the wired public telephone network.

Figure 5.7 depicts the basic topology of a wireless PBX. This topology is for the early systems. As the systems mature, the common control will be part of the PBX. In fact, in the future, all PBXs will have wireless capability as an option that can be ordered by the customer. Most early implementations of wireless PBXs offer voice only. But as we have seen DECT offers a rich data capability; therefore, the standard is poised to provide interesting wide band applications for the office environment when the market is ready.

Now that the spectrum has been allocated in Europe, the United States, and other parts of the world, this industry is ready for rapid growth. One obstacle that needs to be overcome is to understand how these systems fit in with cellular. Will users have to carry two phones, one for cellular and one for the wireless PBX? Or will suppliers make dual mode phones able to handle cellular and cordless? Ideally, the phones would switch to the wireless PBX mode when in the vicinity of

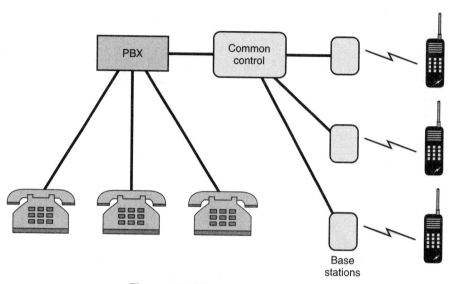

Figure 5.7 Wireless PBX topology.

the PBX, and use cellular only when they have to. While in the PBX domain, there is no charge for air time since the PBX is a private system. Several manufacturers are considering dual mode phones that offer DECT and GSM.

The next system to be discussed is provided by a small company called SpectraLink. It works with an existing PBX, or Centrex. It uses the 900 MHz ISM band that requires no license, but requires that the transmission be spread-spectrum to avoid interfering with the incumbents who do have the primary license for the band. The transmitted power is 100 mw. The topology is shown in Figure 5.8 and is exactly the same as the general one shown in Figure 5.7. The common control is called a Master Control Unit, and the base stations are called Remote Control Units.

The SpectraLink system can cover an area of from 5,000 to 50,000 square feet. The capacity of one MCU is 400 simultaneous calls, or 2,000 phones. The MAC layer implementation is unique. It uses CDMA/TDMA—CDMA to separate the cells and TDMA to channelize within each cell. Using TDMA within the cell to channelize solves the near-far problem without requiring complex agile power control. This is illustrated in Figure 5.9.

Since the phones transmit at different times in the same cell, the problem of one phone so close to the base station saturating it so that it cannot hear a phone near the edge of the cell is an issue the same as in CDMA. CDMA is used to separate the cells, since the signal has to be spread-spectrum anyway to comply with the Part 15 rules of the FCC for ISM bands.

The last wireless PBX system to discuss is an early model offered by Ericsson that was used in the Montreal Olympics. The system also used the ISM bands, since no frequency alloca-

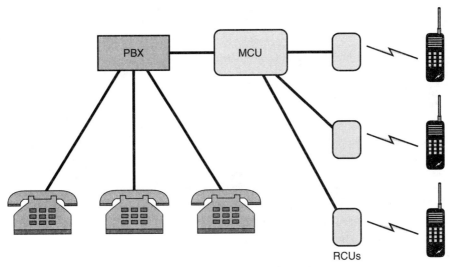

Figure 5.8 SpectraLink configuration.

tion was available then. It used an option of the ISM band, that is not very well known, the low-power option. This option does not require spreading as long as the power is kept very low, on the order of 3 mw. The cells were so small, they had to have about 10 cell sites to cover the Olympic swimming pool.

Ericsson along with all the PBX manufacturers are now manufacturing wireless PBXs like the one mentioned at the beginning of this section, and, in the future, wireless will be an option in all PBXs.

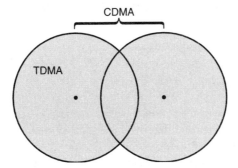

Figure 5.9 CDMA/TDMA implementation.

PHS: Personal Handyphone System

PHS in Japan was aimed from the start to satisfy the needs of:

- Home use
- Office use
- Public access capability
- Wireless local loops.

The standard was developed in Japan by the R&D Center for Radio Systems (RCR) and the Telecommunications Technical Committee (TTC). The potential user base for PHS is estimated at 5.5 million in 1998, and 39 million in 2010. Japan is sure to offer this system in other parts of the world. It has proposed it as one of the PCS standard options in the United States, and succeeded in negotiating with Bellcore to provide a combined proposal, PACS.

The technology of PHS is summarized below:

- FDMA/TDMA/TDD
- 77 FDMA carriers
  - 40 carriers for public systems
  - 1906–1918 MHz = 12 MHz
  - 37 carriers for home/office use
  - 1895–1906 MHz = 11 MHz
- 384 Kbps per carrier
- 4 duplex channels per carrier
- Dynamic channel assignment
- 10 mw average power, 80 mw peak
- 500 mw average power from base station, 4 w peak
- $\pi/4$ DQPSK modulation
- 32 Kbps ADPCM speech coding
- CRC error detection
- Supports low speed mobility.

The MAC and duplexing methods are typical of cordless systems. The frequency allocations are unique in that they divide the band into two parts, one for public use, and one for home/office use. This means that a public system can be collocated with a business system. The carrier is not as wide as that of DECT for only a total of four duplex channels are provided per carrier instead of 12 as in DECT. ADPCM is used in a manner typical of cordless systems. To make better use of the spectrum, quadrature modulation is used. Simple error detection also is used, this, too, is typical of cordless systems that aim at low cost. Finally, low-speed mobility is supported but not vehicular speeds. This is due to the fact that the cell size is small, and the network cannot keep track of a fast-moving mobile that is changing cells at a rapid rate.

PHS provides G3 fax at 4.2 to 7.8 Kbps. It provides modem data at 2.4 to 9.6 Kbps through the speech codec. This means that a regular modem can be used between the computer and the cellular phone, and no special equipment needs to be inserted between the cellular network and the public switched network. A new standard will provide 32 Kbps or 64 Kbps by direct access to one or two bearer channels. In that case, a data set will be needed between the computer and the cellular phone, and a modem will be needed between the cellular network and the analog public-switching network. As the public network migrates to digital, these devices will no longer be needed, and a simple data set will be all that is required.

PACS: Public Access Communication System

PACS is a combination of the Japanese PHS and a system called Wireless Access Communications System that was developed by Bellcore. PACS is one of the proposed low-tier standards for PCS in the United States. It is intended for wireless connectivity to local exchange carriers. It is designed for low-speed portables moving in a small cell system that is served by shoe box sized base stations mounted on telephone poles. The cell sizes are envisioned to be 500 meters or less in size. The characteristics of PACS are similar to other small cell cordless systems. The most notable exception is that it uses Frequency Division Duplexing instead of Time Division Duplexing.

The WACS channelization is summarized by:

- Each carrier has 10 channels, compared with 12 duplex channels for DECT and 4 duplex channels for PHS. WACS is closer to PHS (10 versus 8 total channels), than DECT with 24 total channels
- 32 Kbps ADPCM coding as for DECT and PHS
- Allows lower rate speed codecs in the future
- QPSK modulation, PHS uses π/4 DQPSK, and DECT uses GFSK
- Error detection, no error correction, same for PHS and DECT
- No equalization, same for PHS and DECT.

PACS is a compromise between PHS and WACS. The result is three time slots instead of 10, and π/4 DQPSK modulation. PACS is aimed at:

- Wireless local loops
- Portable public service
- Wireless PBXs.

The frame format for PACS is shown in Figure 5.10.

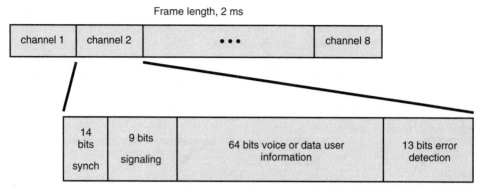

Figure 5.10   PACS frame format.

Since PACS uses FDD, there are two separate frequency allocations. This is how the PCS spectrum is allocated, as we will show shortly. That means that each frame carries traffic in only one direction as with cellular systems. The eight time slots each have the structure shown in the figure. There are 14 bits for synchronization, 9 bits for signaling, and 64 bits for voice or data traffic. Since the frame length is 2 ms, this results in a data rate of 32 Kbps. To end the frame, there are 13 bits for error detection.

Comparison of Cordless Systems and Cellular Systems

Figure 5.11 is a comparison of cordless systems. The regions indicated in Figure 5.11 are where each standard was developed and in the area where it was first proposed and implemented, and where standard will be proposed and implemented in different parts of the world. The bandwidth for PACS is the recently allocated PCS bandwidth in the United States. All the bands are just below 2 GHz except for CT-2. The carrier spacings are comparable except for DECT which is quite high as DECT is aimed at future wide band data applications. The number of carriers and the bit rate correspond to the size of the carrier.

The modulation types are very simple for DECT and CT-2 though a bit more complex for PHS and PACS to obtain a little more data rate from the given allocation. The coding rate is 32 Kbps for all services. The average transmitted power is in the range of 10 mw for all systems. PACS is on the high side, as is the maximum allowed for DECT. The duplexing is all TDD except for PACS that follow the bandwidth allocation.

Figure 5.12 is a comparison of cordless systems with cellular systems. First, and most evident, is the difference in cell sizes. There is a factor difference of about 10 on the small end, and a factor of over 50 on the large end. The impact of this is illustrated later. To serve a large cell, the antenna must be sufficiently high to see over the horizon. This comes into play when selecting sites

System	CT-2	DECT	PHS	PACS
Region	Europe/Asia	Europe	Japan	USA
Frequency band	864–868	1880–1900	1895–1918	1910–1930
Bandwidth (MHz)	20	20	23	120
Spacing (KHz)	100	1728	300	300
Carriers	40	10	77	16/10 MHz
Channels/car	1	12	4	8/pair
Bit rate (Kbps)	72	1152	384	384
Modulation	GFSK	GFSK	$\pi/4$ QPSK	$\pi/4$ QPSK
Coding (Kbps)	32	32	32	32
TX power (mw)	5/10	10/250	10/80	25/200
MAC	FDMA	FDMA/TDMA	FDMA/TDMA	FDMA/TDMA
Duplexing	TDD	TDD	TDD	FDD

Figure 5.11 Comparison of cordless systems.

	Cordless	Cellular
Cell size	Small (50 to 500 m)	Large (0.5 to 30 Km)
Antenna elevation	Low (15 m or less)	High (15 m or more)
Mobility speed	Slow (< 6 Km/hr)	Fast (< 250 Km/hr)
Coverage	Zonal	Ubiquitous
Handset complexity	Low	Moderate
Base complexity	Low	High
Average TX power	2 to 10 mw	100 to 600 mw
Duplexing	TDD	FDD
Coding	32 Kbps ADPCM	8 to 13 Kbps
Error control	CRC	FEC
Multipath mitigation	Antenna diversity	Diversity/equalizer/rake

Figure 5.12 Comparison of cordless and cellular systems.

for locating base stations for each kind of service. Cordless supports pedestrian speeds while cellular supports vehicles traveling on the roads. Cordless systems will have islands of coverage in high density metropolitan areas; cellular has ubiquitous coverage in a whole country. The complexity of the equipment in both the handset and the base station is low for cordless, high for cellular. Cordless base stations are intended to be shoe box size. Cellular base stations need to perform many more functions and thus are larger. Their size will shrink as the components are made smaller, but their complexity will remain higher than their cordless counterparts. The same goes for the handsets. Cellular handsets may be the same size as cordless handsets, but they have to be more complex.

The average transmitted power is a factor of 50 less for cordless than for cellular. That is a large difference from the point of view of battery life and cost. The duplexing method reflects the ease of keeping the systems in synchronization. A smaller cell cordless system is easier to keep in synchronization; therefore, TDD is possible. Coding is simpler for cordless and easier to make equivalent to the wired network. Error handling is simple for cordless; it is usually a simple error detection scheme like Circular Redundancy Check, compared with more sophisticated error correction schemes used for cellular. Finally, multipath is not as much of an issue for cordless systems, and if anything, only antenna diversity is used to mitigate it. In cellular systems it is usually dealt with through the use of equalizers or rake filters.

About the expected coverage of cellular versus PCS systems—as mentioned above, cellular systems are expected to have ubiquitous coverage throughout a country. This does not mean every square meter of a country, but rather most of the areas where people are expected to be normally. And the coverage will start out in the most populated areas and later extend to the less populated areas. The more populated areas are, of course, the downtown areas, the suburbs, and all the major connecting roadways. Initial coverage will not extend to mountainous regions or vacation retreats, for example. This may in fact be a blessing. The situation is illustrated in Figure 5.13.

The densely populated areas and the connecting roadways are covered, but not the whole geography. Smaller cells are used for the cities; larger cells are used for the roadways and sparsely populated areas. If the above country were Germany, there would be numerically many more cells than are shown in the above figure with a service such as GSM and DECT—perhaps 100 times more than are shown. Note also that regulatory agencies specify that the license holder must serve the population that inhabits the area where the license is granted. The regulatory agency does not specify covering the geography, but rather, the population. And the specification does not require 100 percent of the population, but instead a growing percentage over time that reaches a peak of perhaps 95 percent. Making the specification more stringent would render the services too expensive, as the service providers would be forced to build out facilities in extremely sparsely populated areas, where they would not obtain much revenue.

As a last point in the comparison of cordless and cellular systems, it is interesting to put the cell sizes into perspective. Suppose we take the lower limit of the cell sizes in the figure where a cordless system has a cell size 10 times smaller than a cellular system. In that case we have the situation depicted in Figure 5.14. There are about 100 times more cordless cells as there are cellular cells to cover the same area. So it would not be feasible to cover the roadways in a country with cordless cells unless we had thousands of cell sites. And the number of people present in one cell site would not justify the number of channels that would be available in the cell sites. In a downtown area, the number of people and the required channels are consistent with a cordless or PCS system design parameter.

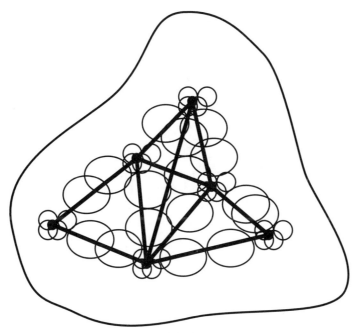

Figure 5.13   Ubiquitous coverage.

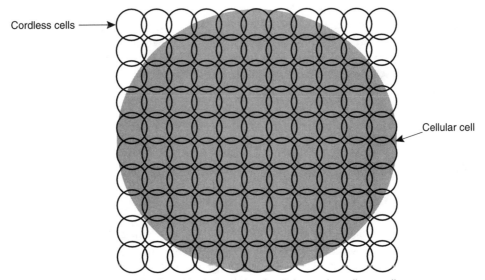

Figure 5.14   Graphical example of cellular and cordless cells.

PCS: Personal Communication Systems

In this section, we discuss PCS spectrum allocations, standards committees, technologies, and standards. PCS has been studied by telephone company research departments for many years. PCS is envisioned to essentially replace the telephony in the future. Its progress will be slow and deliberate, somewhat akin to ISDN. There is much excitement about it now, just like there was about ISDN 10 or 15 years ago when it was first talked about. It is just now that ISDN is finally beginning to appear in volume. The same is likely to happen with PCS. It is a slow very long term evolution of a massive network with many different kinds of uses and huge embedded bases of equipment that cannot be suddenly scrapped and written off. Much of the equipment is part of a rate base of regulated companies that must show reason for removing a piece of equipment that is still providing useful service. So in the same way that the network is becoming digital a decade at a time, so will the march of PCS be, a decade at a time.

It is interesting to look at the words of the FCC as they pertain to PCS. The aim of PCS per the FCC is, "To support small, lightweight wireless telephone sets, and computers that can communicate over the airwaves wherever they are located, and portable facsimile machines and other graphic devices."

The spectrum allocations for PCS, both the licensed part, as well as the unlicensed part are shown in Figure 5.15. There are a total of 60 MHz for the uplink, and 60 MHz for downlink, separated by 20 MHz that is allocated for unlicensed PCS. The licensed parts are divided into six bands: A, B, C, D, E, and F. The A, B, and C bands are 30 MHz each; the D, E, and F bands are 10 MHz each.

The unlicensed PCS allocation is divided into two subbands. One is for asynchronous traffic, or wireless LAN type traffic, the other is for isochronous traffic, or voicelike traffic. Isochronous traffic is the kind of traffic that requires guaranteed bandwidth such as voice, video, or other similar multimedia traffic. The companies who are targeting the isochronous subband are the wireless PBX companies. They are aggressively clearing those bands and readying them for use for wireless PBXs. The asynchronous band is meeting some difficulties. The computer companies are not as aggressively pursuing the clearing of that band. Ironically, it was they, in particular Apple Computer, who started the process of lobbying the FCC for these bands. They were looking for a band where wireless LANs could enjoy primary status instead of being relegated to secondary status in the ISM bands. The telephony companies have more experience and feel more at ease with matters relating to regulatory and government agencies and are having more success utilizing the unlicensed PCS bands.

The A, B, and C blocks were the first to be auctioned off to the industry. It was the first such major auction of spectrum, and it yielded over $7 billion in revenue to the U.S. government. It is estimated that it would cost about $20 billion to build out a PCS system in those bands, so the cost of the spectrum is a substantial portion of the total cost of the system. In effect, it becomes a 25 percent tax on the system and its users.

This is the first major spectrum auction, but it is for sure not the last, not in the United States, and not in the world. Already, the U.S. government has plans to auction additional spectrum. In

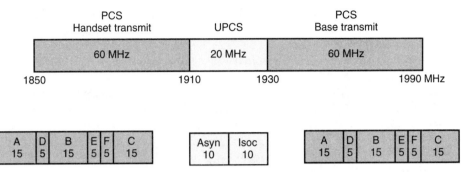

Figure 5.15 PCS spectrum allocations.

fact, it is doubtful that any spectrum will be released by any other means from now on. Moreover, this trend is beginning in other parts of the world. Large PCS suppliers are speaking to other governments about obtaining spectrum in their countries in the same way. The lure of the revenue to the governments of these countries is hard to resist.

The auctioning of spectrum is changing the landscape of the telecommunications industry. The total impact is still to be seen. One effect is that it is causing a reconsolidation of the industry. For example, in the United States, the parts of the Bell System seem to be coming back together again to be able to bid and win large, expensive spectrum auctions. Most of the A, B, and C blocks were won by three or four major consortia of companies.

In addition to paying for the spectrum initially, a service provider must then contend with relocating incumbents who have licenses in those bands. The bands are not empty. The FCC allocated the bands to the PCS industry, provided they help relocate the incumbents to higher bands that the FCC has identified. This process can lead to some incumbents seizing the opportunity to generate some extra revenue. On the whole it is proceeding smoothly, with some minor exceptions that may lead to a generation of extra rules by the FCC to prevent taking advantage of the situation. This is what is holding back the utilization of the UPCS bands, particularly for the computer companies and the asynchronous part of the band. It takes an organized effort of the industry to clear the band, and the computer industry has not been able to muster such organization to date.

The term of a PCS license is 10 years with renewal provisions similar to cellular. A PCS license holder must actively build out the network to serve the population in the areas where he holds the license. He cannot hold on to the license and do nothing. The build-out schedule is fairly aggressive as seen below:

- Serve 1/3 of the population in each market area within five years of being licensed
- Serve 2/3 of the population within seven years
- Serve 90 percent of the population within ten years.

It may be easy to serve 1/3 of the population within the first five years. One-third of the population probably inhabits a small fraction of the geography. It becomes harder and harder to serve the rest of the population that may be scattered throughout the rest of the geography. But at least the service provider will be producing revenue from the first 1/3 to help finance the build-out of the remaining parts of the network.

We have had two service providers for cellular for some time in the United States. The price of service has fluctuated slightly. The terminal prices were dropped but the air time has remained fairly stable. It seems that two service providers are not enough to stimulate aggressive pricing. When PCS was first being discussed by the FCC and the industry through the process of inquiry and comment, the FCC suggested three or four competitors. This was incrementally more than the two that were allowed with cellular. The industry came back requesting up to six competitors. They settled on five. This should create very aggressive pricing. The issue may be whether service providers with shallower pockets will be able to stay in business as the deeper pockets are competing for market share.

There is also a price of competition that stems from the inefficiency of splintering trunk groups. With one service provider, all the traffic is offered to one group of channels. With two, some of the traffic is offered to half of the channels; the rest of the traffic is offered to the other half of the channels. This causes the total amount of traffic that can be handled to drop. When there are three service providers, even less traffic can be handled, and so on. Figure 5.16 illustrates this effect. The assumptions behind this table are:

- 1 user per 10 m^2
- 0.2 Erlang per user
- Antenna separation = 40 m
- Cell size = 1,366 m^2
- Traffic, cell = 27.3 Erlang
- Channels/cell = 34
- Bandwidth = 40 MHz.

Carriers	1	2	3	4
Traffic/carrier	24E	12E	8E	6E
Channels/cells	35	20	15	13
Spectrum/carrier	42 MHz	24 MHz	18 MHz	16 MHz
Total Spectrum	42 MHz	48 MHz	54 MHz	64 MHz
Increase	Reference	14 percent	29 percent	52 percent

Figure 5.16 Traffic throughput for multiple service providers.

As the figure shows, the amount of spectrum needed for this example with four service providers is 52 percent more than with one service provider. This effect can be ameliorated if the service providers agree to build out the facilities and then offer their channels to any users regardless of which service provider they originally signed up with. This is unlikely in the short term. If it were possible, it would require a sophisticated revenue sharing plan, and would mean that all service providers use the same standard, or have a complex interfacing scheme.

For the foreseeable future, when a person signs up with a service provider, they will be able to use the facilities of just that service provider in a given region. If they roam to another area, they will be able to use the facilities of other service providers if they use the same standard. With three to seven PCS standards, the likelihood of having the same standard is not high. This means that even if one service provider has empty channels, while the one that the person is signed up with has no free channels, the person has to wait for service until his service provider has a free channel. That is the essence behind trunk group splintering. It is also the problem with having so many standards. The advantage of having so many standards is, of course, that the competition will result in a market tested and proven standard that will be robust, the king of the hill after surviving in real-life combat. This is the American way. It seems to be working just fine.

The United States is divided into what are called Major Trading Areas and Basic Trading Areas. The MTAs are the big metropolitan areas such as New York, Chicago, Los Angeles, and so on. There are 51 MTAs in the United States. By contrast, there are 492 BTAs. These are the smaller municipalities. Licenses are awarded for MTAs and BTAs, along with blocks A, B, C, D, E, and F. The FCC specifies the frequency bands, and the maximum power that can be transmitted in those bands, but does not specify what standard the provider should use. The license holder can use any standard, or his own proprietary standard, if he so wishes along as he satisfies the power and frequency limits. The industry meets in various committees to determine what standards it would like to follow, but still it is not a requirement that a license holder use any of the standards produced by the standards body.

The PCS and Cellular Standards Bodies in the United States

The T1 committee is a large standards organization that is responsible for the production of most of the telecommunications standards in the United States. It has produced standards for digital transmission, Signaling System 7, and ISDN. It is now very active in the setting of standards for Wireless Networking. The various T1 committees and their functions are:

- T1A1—Performance
- T1E1—Network interfaces
- T1M1—Operations, administration, maintenance, and provisioning
- T1P1—Systems engineering, standards planning, and program management

- T1S1—Service architectures and signaling
- T1X1—Digital hierarchy and synchronization.

All these committees are involved to some extent in Wireless Networking. T1P1 is involved in the management of the process across all these committees and in other organizations outside of T1. It has subcommittees as follows:

- T1P1.1—Standards planning and program management
- T1P1.2—Wireless access
- T1P1.3—Service and architectures, numbering plan.

T1E1 works on user to public network interfaces. It is responsible for the development of the air interface for PCS in its subcommittee T1E1.9. It interfaces with T1P1 regarding the services to be supported, and the system objectives.

The TR45 committee is a different body from the T1 group. TR 45 is composed of cellular carriers and generates cellular standards such AMPS, the different kinds of digital cellular standards, and now PCS standards. The subentities of TR45 are shown in Figure 5.17.

TR45.1 is where AMPS, and later narrow-band AMPS were developed. TR45.2 is responsible for intersystem operation, for example, the IS41 standard for interoperating among cellular providers. TR45.3 generated IS 54, the digital cellular TDMA standard, and later IS 136, the more advanced digital cellular TDMA standard that has short messaging, closed user groups, and so on. TR45.5 is responsible for the CDMA standard IS 95, and other wide band standards. The remaining two subcommittees are involved with microcell and with PCS.

These subcommittees work in areas that are very closely tied with the work of T1E1.9. For this reason, the three entities decided to meet jointly to hammer out a joint air interface. That body is called the Joint Technical Committee whose composition and responsibilities are summarized below:

- Joint technical committee composition
  - T1E1.9
  - TR45.4
  - TR45.6

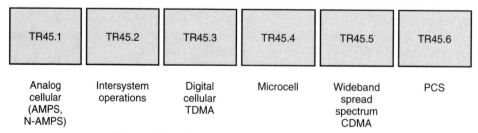

Figure 5.17   TR45 cellular standards committee.

- Scope of work
  - Develop a common physical layer needed to establish a wireless interface between a user set and network radio port in the 850 to 1900 MHz band.

There is also a standard called TR 41 that is aimed at wireless PBXs. A front runner proposal for this standard is the DECT standard. DECT has a good chance of succeeding in the United States because U.S. chip manufacturers make DECT chip sets. It is difficult for a standard that is developed in another country to succeed if it means no revenue for the local companies. On the other hand, if local companies have a good chance in sharing in the profit brought about by a good standard, it will flourish. We have seen this occur in the auto industry as more and more foreign makes began to manufacture their product in the United States.

Standards Bodies in Europe

In Europe, we have CEPT, which is the Conference of European PTs. It is the regulatory agency in Europe. It is similar to the FCC in the United States. It allocates spectrum, and sometimes defines a coexistence standard. When a more complex interoperability standard is required, it delegates that work to ETSI, which we will discuss shortly. For example, in the case of CT-1, the cordless phone system in Europe, CEPT defined a simple coexistence standard. In the case of GSM and DECT, CEPT delegated that development of a comprehensive standard to the appropriate body within ETSI.

The European Telecommunications Standards Institute (ETSI), is similar to T1 and IEEE in the United States. There is also the European Computer Manufacturers Association, which is similar to the TR45 committee in the United States. ETSI has 12 subcommittees:

1. Network aspects
2. Business telecommunications
3. Signaling protocols and switching
4. Transmission and multiplexing
5. Terminal equipment
6. Equipment engineering
7. Radio equipment and systems (RES)
8. Special Mobile Group (GSM)
9. Paging systems
10. Satellite earth stations
11. Advanced testing methods
12. Human factors

The ones of most interest here are the GSM and the RES subcommittees. RES has several entities:

RES 1

Maritime mobile

RES 2

Land mobile

RES 3

Wireless PBX, DECT

. . .

RES 10

Wireless LANs.

The ones of interest are RES 3 for DECT, and RES 10 for Wireless LANs.

The Japanese environment has a similar structure to the United States and to the European structures. There is the Ministry of Public Telecommunications, which is the regulatory agency. The Institute of Electronic and Information Engineers is a standard committee obviously similar to the IEEE in the United States. There are committees such as the Telecommunications Technology Council that works on frequency sharing plans, and the Wireless LAN system committee.

This is the standards picture in the major areas. The U.S. standards bodies are very open. Anyone can attend. Anyone can obtain copies of the documents. Anyone can make proposals, and indeed they do. The European standards bodies are not quite as open, and the Japanese standards bodies are the most difficult to participate in. There are, of course, also international standards bodies such as CCITT. Representatives from T1 and from ETSI, and from all over the world attend the international standards committees. They return to the committees in their homeland and decide how closely to follow the international standard. And if they decide not to follow it exactly, they decide how to interface to it. In the case of the T1 committee, they follow the standard quite closely, but not exactly. They follow it closely enough so that in many cases they generate delta documents to the CCITT documents instead of totally separate documents.

The standards that are generated in the United States, Europe, and Asia are spread through the rest of the world via proposals by the companies who helped develop them and who are interested in offering the service in other countries. The picture that emerges is a patchwork of different standards from different parts of the world with interconnection agreements and revenue sharing plans.

PCS Technologies

Now let us turn to the technologies behind PCS, in particular:

- The network components
- The digital cordless terminal

- Network interfaces
- Data capabilities
- The original vision of PCS.

First, let us examine the concept of personal mobility and how it is related to terminal mobility. Personal mobility is the ability of the user to access the services he subscribes to from any terminal, on the basis of a unique Universal Personal Telecommunications (UPT) number, whether from a wired terminal or a wireless terminal. And it is the ability of the network to provide the service to the user, locate him at any point in time, and of course, charge him for the service. For example, a user may be in a hotel room; he would call in to let the network know at which terminal he is located. In this case it is a wired terminal. All calls destined for that user would dial his UPT number. They would reach the user in that hotel room; until such time when the user informs the network that he is at another location.

The amount of work to provide personal mobility to users is significant. It is not as visible as the terminal mobility that we will discuss shortly, but in some ways it is more complex.

Terminal mobility is the ability of the user's wireless terminal to move while accessing and using services. And it is the ability of the network to maintain the connection and to keep track of the user. This is the part that is most visible and that receives the most attention. Personal mobility and terminal mobility are contrasted in Figure 5.18. Personal mobility includes the UPT number, the service profile that describes the services the user has subscribed to. It can be accessed from any terminal, wired or wireless. Terminal mobility meets the needs of moving terminals as well as mobile terminals. Moving terminals are defined as to be able to move with pedestrian speeds; mobile terminals can move with vehicular speeds. Moving terminals use a small cell system like PCS; mobile terminals use a cellular system. Mobile terminals cannot use a small cell PCS network, because they would be changing cells too quickly; therefore, the network would not be able to keep track of them fast enough.

Figure 5.19 depicts the steps that take place in completing a call. Suppose that Bill is from Helsinki, and he is visiting Munich. He is the calling party. Suppose that Sabina is from London,

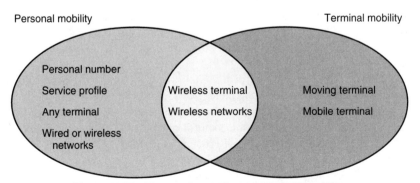

Figure 5.18 Personal mobility and terminal mobility.

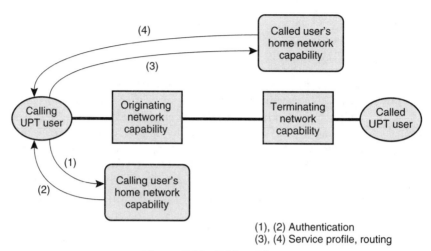

(1), (2) Authentication
(3), (4) Service profile, routing

Figure 5.19   PCS call flow.

and she is visiting Stockholm. Bill wants to call Sabina. He dials her number and presses the send button. The first thing that must happen is for him to become authenticated. A signal goes from the Munich switch to Bill's HLR in Helsinki to check his good standing with his cellular company. If he has registered with them and he has paid his bill, a signal comes back from Helsinki to Munich authenticating Bill. The number he dialed for Mary then goes to Mary's home network operator, her HLR in London. That HLR indicates that Mary is not at home in London, she is visiting Stockholm. The Munich switch then sets up the call from Munich to Stockholm.

The bill for the call is shared between Bill and Sabina according to a fair algorithm that allocates cost according to the cost of carrying the call, and what Bill and Sabina expect to pay. For example, Bill expects to catch Sabina in London, but she was in Stockholm. Sabina was supposed to be in London, but she is in Stockholm receiving calls. It is not a simple matter how to allocate the cost of the call. At the moment, different network operators allocate the cost in different ways. Some ways do not make much sense at the present time. Not only that, but in many cases the calls are routed in very nonoptimum ways, including triangle routing and back and forth routing. This is a short term phenomenon, and will be smoothed out as time goes on, and operators streamline their interworking.

Figure 5.20 shows the components of a digital handset. Examining these components, we can see how a cellular handset and a PCS handset would differ. First, we have the power subsystem. This is the battery and power supply, with intelligent power management to conserve battery life. The antenna subsystem may provide some sort of diversity. The Radio Frequency subsystem is the front end of the receiver. Digital Signal Processors perform RF functions as well as audio functions. They implement the Common Air Interface, perform synchronization, clocking, and Analog to Digital conversion. The audio DSP functions include the voice coder and decoders, the

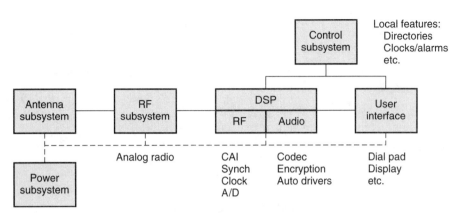

Figure 5.20 Digital handset structure.

encryption, and audio drivers. DSPs play an important role in digital handsets. The user interface circuits handle the dial pad, the display, and other user functions. The control subsystem is where personal speed call lists, clocks, and alarms reside.

Cellular handsets are very small in size. PCS handsets cannot be much smaller, unless they are implemented in a different form factor, such as the ATT watch phone. Where a cellular handset and a PCS handset differ is in the complexity of the various circuits. For example, a cellular handset must implement a complex vocoder, whereas a PCS phone uses comparatively simple ADPCM. The CAI for cellular is more complex than that for PCS. The power transmitted by a cellular phone is over 100 times greater than for a PCS phone. Cellular phones have to use equalizers or rake filters to mitigate multipath; PCS phones do not. Next we turn to the PCS standards that are proposed in the United States, compare them, and discuss which will be implemented first and why.

PCS Standards

As we considered in an earlier section, the Joint Technical Committee of TR45 representatives and T1 representatives met intensively to produce a common air interface for PCS. Eight proposals were submitted to the JTC. The proposers were asked to compromise and reduce the number of proposals; the result was a reduction from eight to seven! And the two entities that compromised were the largest two: ATT and Japan! So we have seven standards for PCS. It will be left up to the market to decide which of the standards are winners. We will present the seven standards, and then discuss which are most likely to be implemented first.

The standards fall into two tiers: high tier and low tier. The two tiers are distinguished by:

- High tier
  - Larger cells, smaller than cellular but not as small as the cordless cells we have discussed
  - Support vehicular mobility
  - These standards are similar to cellular with smaller cells
- Low tier
  - Small cells like the cordless cells we discussed
  - Support pedestrian speeds
  - Low-power handsets and base stations
  - These standards are similar to cordless.

The seven standards and which tier they are in are shown in Figure 5.21. The three high-tier standards are derived from the TDMA standard, the CDMA standard, and GSM/DCS standard. The low-tier standards are the PACS standard already discussed, a DECT based standard, and two new standards that use wide band CDMA. The cellular-based standards are up-banded versions of their cellular cousins. IS-54 is up-banded from 800 MHz to 1.9 GHz, the same for CDMA, and the DCS based standard is up-banded from the 1.8-GHz band in Europe to the 1.9-GHz band in the United States.

The DECT based standard is DECT modified to work in indoor as well as outdoor environments. The wide band CDMA standards are based on new experiments with this technology. PACS is based on several years of research in Bellcore, combined with the PHS work in Japan on small cell high density systems.

The high-tier standards offer easy interoperation with their cellular counterparts. They essentially represent the cellular carriers using the new PCS bands to build slightly smaller cell cellular systems to meet new demand. The IS-54 PCS standard would work easily with the IS-54 cellular

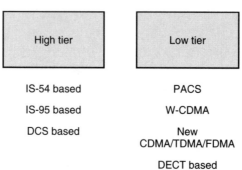

Figure 5.21 The seven PCS standards.

standard. It would be relatively easy to build handsets and base stations that can handle both standards. The same would apply to the IS-95 based standard and IS-95 cellular, and with the DCS based standard and a GSM cellular network.

The W-CDMA standard is based on experiments by InterDigital and OKI Electronics. It uses the full 5-MHz bandwidth of a small PCS allocation. It claims to work with both large cells as well as small cells. The CDMA/RDMA/FDMA standard is based on a Pioneer Preference system by Omnipoint. It also uses the full 5 MHz bandwidth of a small PCS allocation. It provides 32, 8-Kbps time slots, and can support up to 52 Kbps of data. It requires no equalizers. As would be expected, the DECT based standard is particularly well suited for indoor environments.

The seven PCS standards are compared in Figures 5.22 and 5.23 for the high-tier standards and the low-tier standards, respectively.

The three high-tier standards use FDD as is typical of cellular. The bandwidth of the carrier is 30 KHz for the IS-54 based standard since it is derived from the analog AMPS standard. The DCS based standard has 200 KHz as does GSM. The CDMA standard has the 1.25 MHz bandwidth that allows it to use spread-spectrum to produce 64 orthogonal channels.

The channels per carrier are three for TDMA and eight for DCS consistent with the protocols they are based on. The efficiency relative to AMPS is x3 for TDMA since three TDMA channels are derived from each FDMA AMPS channel. DCS states x2-3 efficiency, which is a conservative

	IS-54 based	IS-95 based	DCS based
MAC	TDMA	CDMA	TDMA
Duplexing	FDD	FDD	FDD
Carrier BW	30 KHz	1.25 MHz	200 KHz
Channels/carrier	3	20	8
x AMPS	x3	x10	x2-3
Modulation	$\pi/4$ DQPSK	QPSK	GMSK
Frequency reuse	7	1	4
Power	100 mw	200 mw	125 mw
Frame length	40 ms	20 ms	4.615 ms
Equalizer	yes	Rake filters	yes
Vocoder	8/4 Kbps	8/4/2/1 Kbps	13/6.5 Kbps

Figure 5.22 The PCS high tier standards.

	PACS	New	W-CDMA	DECT based
MAC	TDMA	CDMA/TDMA	W-CDMA	TDMA
Duplexing	FDD	TDD	FDD	TDD
Carrier BW	300 KHz	5 MHz	5 MHz	1728 KHz
Channels/carrier	8	32	128	12
x AMPS	x0.8	x16	x16	x0.2
Modulation	π/4 DQPSK	CPQPSK	QPSK	GFSK
Frequency reuse	7	3	1	9
Power	100 mw		500 mw	20.8 mw
Frame length	40 ms	20 ms		10 ms
Equalizer	yes	no	no	no
Vocoder	32 Kbps	8 Kbps	32 Kbps	32 Kbps

Figure 5.23   The PCS low-tier standards.

estimate. Since DCS, like GSM, does power control, and even stops transmission when the speaker is silent, the amount of interference is minimized, and the system should be capable of greater bandwidth efficiency. CDMA claims x10 efficiency. This is based on a reuse factor of 1. It remains to be seen whether such a reuse factor is possible with the early systems. Theoretically, it is possible; however, early implementation had a hard time achieving this goal. If it does use a reuse factor of seven, then the bandwidth efficiency of CDMA becomes 10/7, or x1.4 AMPS.

The power of all three high-tier systems is the range of 100 to 200 mw. The TDMA systems require equalization; CDMA uses rake filtering. The vocoding rates are a bit higher for the DCS based standard. CDMA claims the ability to drop all the way to 1 Kbps in the future.

The low-tier standards are compared in Figure 5.23. PACS and DECT are TDMA based. The other two are wide band CDMA based. They all use TDD that is typical of cordless systems except for PACS that uses FDD. This is because PACS uses the pair of PCS allocations for the two different directions of transmission for which they were intended. The other standards use each band for both directions of transmission, and use TDD in each of the bands. There is no reason not to do this. With FDD we require two separate bands, with TDD we do not.

The carrier bandwidth is narrowest for PACS in this group. PACS is most like the high-tier standards in this respect. The other three including DECT are wide band. They are capable of greater ultimate data throughput. DECT can provide up to over ½ Mbps. The wide band CDMA systems can provide data in that range as well. PACS will be limited to data rates in the range of 250 Kbps. PACS was based on work from some years ago, and may be showing its age before it reaches the limelight.

All low-tier systems use the wire line coding rate of 32 Kbps except for the CDMA/TDMA standard. The spectral efficiency of the low-tier systems varies greatly. PACS and DECT are quite low, whereas the wide band CDMA systems claim very large efficiency factors. Those will have to be borne out by actual large-scale implementations. The power levels vary significantly in the low-tier systems. DECT's average is the lowest; W-CDMA is highest. PACS is the only standard that uses equalization.

Wireless Loops

First, we need to define what is meant by wireless local loops. There has always been a rural, small capacity point-to-point system for reaching the farmhouse that is far away from any population center. For such a house, it was most economical to use radio as opposed to wire. At the house, the radio was terminated into a jack in the wall, and the rest was wired. This is depicted in Figure 5.24.

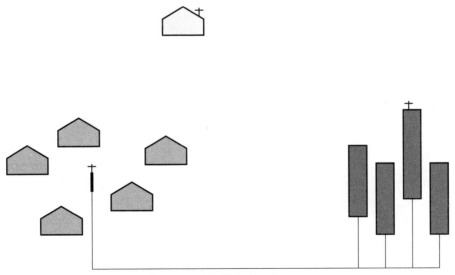

Figure 5.24 Wireless loops.

What about the local suburb with housing developments? Here, we have a number of options. For most countries in North America and Europe, most houses have wired service already. This is not the case in many countries where the wired telephone penetration is less than 5 percent. In those countries, it sometimes is most economical to go directly to wireless loops. This is the situation depicted in Figure 5.24. The area is covered with PCS base stations, and the users have PCS phones that are able to roam about their house with, or they can go to the downtown area that is also equipped with PCS cell sites and use them there as well. This kind of wireless loop is being considered, for example, to serve new condominium complexes in Malaysia, and other similar applications.

What about the areas where we already have wired service? Will new wireless systems replace the wired service? Most people would argue that the answer to that question is no. Wired service will provide greater and greater bandwidth, for example through basic rate ISDN first, and then primary rate ISDN. Wireless will supplement the wired high bandwidth network and offer users freedom of movement for most of the applications that do not require great amounts of bandwidth. So, for normal communications, the users would rely on their wireless terminal, but when it comes to shopping at home, or entertainment on demand, or other high bandwidth applications, they would rely on the wired network and the large screen with the set top box helping to navigate the network. For those cases, we will have the medium-bandwidth wireless loops as shown in Figure 5.25, as well as the existing wiring enhanced to provide wide band ISDN services.

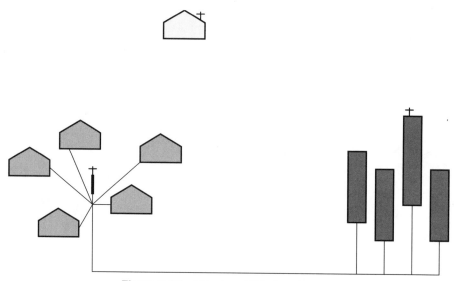

Figure 5.25 Wired and Wireless Loops.

Discussion of Cellular, Microcellular, and PCS

Another way to look at the relationship between cellular and PCS is to see how much of the population can be supported by the frequency bands allocated to each. For the United States, this yields:

- Current cellular penetration is 10 percent in metropolitan areas
- Demand is growing to about 40 percent in the next 10 years
- Current analog cellular can grow to meet 7 percent penetration. That is why it is necessary to implement digital in metropolitan areas
- Digital cellular can grow to meet 25 percent penetration
- PCS can grow to handle almost 100 percent penetration.

As we have discussed, the migration from cellular to PCS will not be in one step. We will go through a phase of small-cell cellular provided by the high-tier PCS standards such as DCS 1900. This gradual migration makes sense, since it would be a daunting task to put in the number of cells required to provide good coverage with a very small-cell system such as PCS. After the high-tier systems are in place and producing revenue, and the system design is honed, then we can put in the higher density systems with the greater number of base stations.

We have spoken about many different kinds of services. Figure 5.26 summarizes them. In this figure the applications are in the middle and range from wireless PBXs and local networks for private business applications, to wireless local loops, to telepoint for high-density public areas, to residential cordless. Four levels of mobility are identified from local to regional to national to international. There are solid lines that indicate which technology definitely applies to what applications, but there are also many dotted lines that are not shown. For example, DECT/PCS systems definitely apply to wireless PBXs, local networks, telepoint and wireless loops, and residential cordless. Cellular applies to mobility at all levels. Microcellular, or high-tier PCS, apply to the intermediate systems ranging from telepoint to local loops, residential cordless, and local and regional mobility. The dotted lines would include applying microcellular to national coverage. Some suppliers have plans of covering nations with DCS 1800 technology. Others are considering using microcellular for business applications.

We have also spoken of many different sizes of cells. In Figure 5.27, we suggest a classification. Cells larger than 50 Km in radius are the realm of satellite systems. The next three categories encompass cellular systems of varying applications. The large cell systems are for rural areas with cell sizes from 10 Km to 50 Km in radii. Most cellular systems have radii from 1 to 10 Km in size and serve urban areas. Minicells that have radii that range from 100 m to 1,000 m can be used to provide service to dense urban areas. Both cellular systems as well as high-tier PCS systems can be used in these cases. This is an area of overlap between the different systems. Microcell systems serve office campuses and office buildings. The cell sizes are in the 10 m to 100 m range. This is

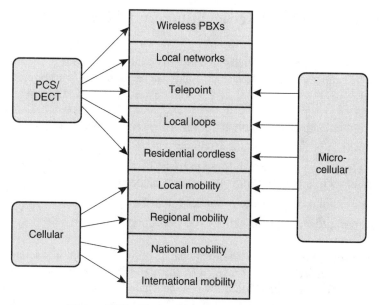

Figure 5.26   Technology mapping to markets.

Cell type	Cell radius	Coverage	Services
Huge cell	> 50 Km	Continents	Satellite
Large cell	10–50 Km	Rural	Cellular
Cell	1–10 Km	Urban	Cellular
Minicell	100–1000 m	Dense urban	Cellular/PCS DECT
Microcell	10–100 m	Office campus	DECT/PCS Radio LANs
Pico cell	2–10 m	Single room	IR LANs
Femto cell	< 2 m	Private short range	IRDA

Figure 5.27   Cell size classification.

quite a small cell for a cellular system, it is the area where low-tier PCS systems shine, and cordless systems are most suited. This area is where wireless PBXs will be applied.

This is the size of cells for Wireless LANs as well. The kind of Wireless LANs that have this kind of cell size are usually radio based. There are also infrared Wireless LANs. Their range is smaller and fits in the picocell category. These systems serve a single room, not only because their range is limited, but also because infrared cannot penetrate walls. We are still not at the end. There is one more category that will become very prevalent, the femto cell category for private, point-to-point infrared systems. There is a standard that was developed by the Infra Red Data Association. The association was led by HP, and produced the first phase of the standard for very short range, 2 m or less transmission between two end systems. This kind of system is very low cost and will be found in the majority of notebook computers in the future.

Future Systems

Future cellular and PCS systems are sometimes called third-generation systems. The three generations are:

- First generation
  - Analog cellular: AMPS, NMT, TACS
  - Analog cordless: CT-0, CT-1, U.S. analog, Japanese analog cellular
- Second generation
  - Digital cellular: GSM/DCS, TDMA, CDMA
  - Digital cordless: CT-2, DECT, PCS standards
- Third generation
  - FPLMTS: Future Public Land Mobile Telecommunications System
  - IMT-2000: International Mobile Telecommunications 2000
  - UMTS: Universal Mobile Telecommunications Systems.

The evolution from first generation to second generation in the case of GSM was not evolutionary. There were not many installed analog cellular systems in Europe, so there was not much motivation to make the new digital standard backwards compatible with them. In the United States, the amount of analog cellular was significant and is likely to remain useful for some time, so backward compatibility and interoperability were made part of the standard. The new digital cordless and PCS systems do not bother with backward compatibility with existing analog cordless systems not because there are not great numbers of them, but because they are relatively cheap, and they do not adhere to any standard. They are mostly proprietary.

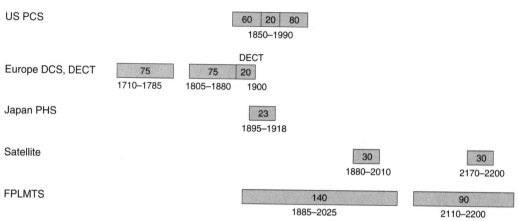

Figure 5.28   Frequency allocations near 2 GHz.

The case in going from second to third generation is different. There will be a huge invest-ment in digital second generation systems by that time, and the evolution to third generation sys-tems must be smooth. The third generation is differentiated from second generation systems in three major areas: frequency, cell size, and data rate. Future systems will be at higher frequencies where there is more bandwidth available. They will have smaller cell sizes to provide higher user densities, and they will provide higher data throughput for future multimedia wireless applications. FPLMTS is envisioned to provide data rates up to 2 Mbps for voice, data, and video traffic, with bursts up to 20 Mbps for high-speed wireless LANS. The World Association for Radio Communi-cations earmarked the following bands for FPLMTS:

- 1885–2025 MHz = 140 MHz
- 2110–2200 MHz = 90 MHz.

This allocation is compared to the frequency allocations for cellular and PCS near 2 GHz in Figure 2.28. The allocations are drawn roughly to scale. The PCS spectrum is a total of 140 MHz. DCS is 150 MHz with another 20 MHz for DECT. The FPLMTS bands are not actual allocations, but rather suggested areas by WARC for future harmonization of allocations throughout the world, so users can roam and the handsets can operate by fine-tuning of frequency.

Summary

By way of summary, Figure 5.29 presents the basic components of a cellular or PCS system. The handheld talks to the base station. The base station is connected to the wireless interfaces that include the Base Station Controller and the Mobile Switching Center. The MSC is connected to the Public Switched Network. Figure 5.30 shows the variety of wireless connections that can exist.

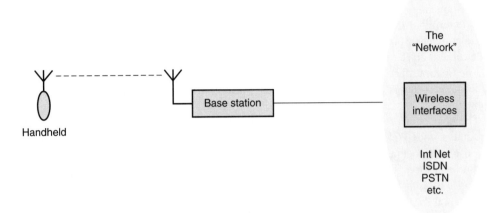

Figure 5.29   Network components.

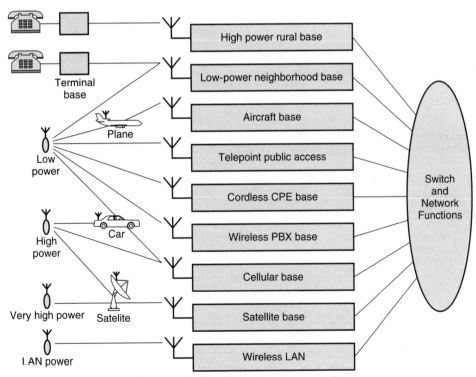

Figure 5.30   Possible wireless connections.

This kind of picture was discussed in the process of developing the PCS standards in order to achieve as much harmony among the different scenarios as possible. It may not be possible to have one single terminal to be able to connect to all the different interfaces, but perhaps we can minimize the number of possible interfaces to stay close to the vision of having a single terminal that provides ubiquitous coverage.

The first interface at the top of the figure is an interface—the high power rural interface. This is the farmhouse that is far away from any other connections. This interface has been in existence for some time.

The next interface is the low-power neighborhood base. This would serve a community of houses and provide PCS service to those houses. That means that everyone in each house would be able to use a PCS phone in his house and in the whole neighborhood. This would effectively replace the local loop. This would also replace cordless phones. We will be able to have as many PCS phones in each house as we would like. Each person could have one, or some could share a single terminal. Each person would then have his own number that goes with him wherever he is.

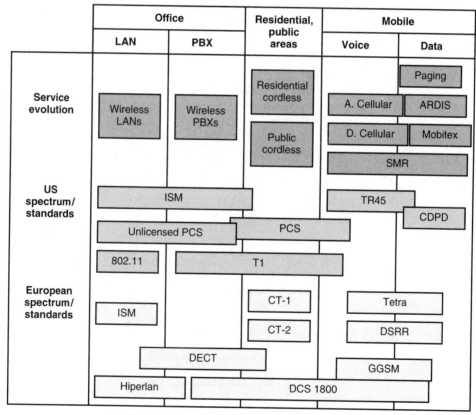

Figure 5.31   Wireless Networking activities.

We would serve the suburban community with the low-power neighborhood interface and the downtown area with the telepoint public access interface in the streets and in public areas. We could be in an office building and be served by a PBX, or other Customer Premises Equipment, in which case, we would hopefully be using a standard in the PBX that is compatible with the PCS service we are using elsewhere.

If we are in the car, traveling at high speeds, we would not be able to use the very small-cell PCS systems, so we must switch to a cellular infrastructure. But do we have to switch to a different handset as well? Not necessarily, the trend is to build dual-mode handsets that would handle both situations. One common combination is cellular/PCS, for example, GSM/DECT. Another possibility is to have a relay in the car that would accept as input the PCS handset, but connect to the cellular network.

And if we are in an airplane, do we have to switch off all our cellular and PCS equipment and use yet another system? Or is it possible to have a PCS base station in the plane, appropriately designed so as not to interfere with the sensitive navigation equipment of the plane, and yet allow us to use our PCS phone to connect to the phone network below.

The cellular interface in Figure 5.30 is referred to as the high power interface. By high power, we mean the 0.6 to 2 watt range that is used in cellular systems. It is high relative to the low-power PCS set that has an average in the range of 10 mw. We also have satellite terminals that could be connected to a LEO system, and finally to a LAN interface.

The primary responsibility of the phone company as far as the PCS standards are concerned is the low-power neighborhood interface and the telepoint interface. This is what the PCS standards are aimed at primarily, but it is helpful to see the whole picture to minimize the number of interfaces we will eventually have.

So, now we have discussed the middle three columns of Figure 5.31, which is reproduced here for convenience.

The only area not yet discussed is mobile radio, which is the subject for the next chapter. In this chapter, we discussed cordless telephony and PCS. We started with the roots of cordless telephony in the present widespread analog cordless phones we all have in our homes. We then discussed CT-2, CT-2+, DECT, and PHS. Then we looked at PCS, the frequency allocations for it, the seven proposed standards, and how they compare. Then, we discussed wireless loops, and future third-generation systems. In the next chapter, we will discuss mobile radio systems.

6

Mobile Radio Systems

The market for mobile radio is in the process of structural change from a private systems market to one that mixes the supply of private systems with the provision of public services. In this chapter, we discuss:

- Applications of Private Mobile Radio, and Public Access Mobile Radio, and how they relate to cellular
- Relationship of PMR and PAMR systems with Specialized Mobile Radio and Enhance Specialized Mobile Radio systems
- Mobile radio technologies
  - Private systems—small, medium, and large
  - Public systems
- The Digital Short Range Radio standard for PMR
- The Tetra standard for PAMR
- Supply chain for mobile radio.

Historical Perspective of Mobile Radio

Mobile radio is the oldest form of Wireless Networking. It has been serving police departments, fire departments, ambulance fleets, airport operation staffs, security staffs, truck fleets, and many other vertical applications for many years. Most of these systems used voice to perform their functions. They used a variety of vehicle-mounted units as well as hand-held "walkie talkie" units. Most of the systems were private. The police department or airport operations staff obtained a license to operate their systems in a specific area. No one else used that frequency band in that area.

This guaranteed the group that they would have their channels when they were needed. For example, in case of an emergency when many fire trucks and fire fighting personnel were required in a specific area, the fire department would be assured of having their channels available to handle the emergency. This provided a guarantee but at the price of having these channels going unused at times when some other group could be using them.

Simple mobile radio systems used a single channel. Everyone shared this channel, and had to wait his turn to send his message. For example, the taxicab company had a dispatcher who spoke to taxicabs one at a time to dispatch them and otherwise relay messages to them. In most cases, the traffic pattern was like that of the taxicab company, from a central control point to the mobiles in the field. Mobile-to-mobile communications were not possible, and in fact, the way the system was run, it was not usually necessary.

More sophisticated mobile radio systems are trunked—this means that they have multiple channels. In this case, there is usually one channel that is designated as a "meet me" channel. People would meet at that channel and agree to switch to one of the free channels to carry out their conversation. This is done manually in the medium-size systems, and automatically in the larger systems where the equipment does the meet-me function, and then switches to a free channel available to the user.

The terminals varied a great deal. One supplier's approach to terminals is:

- Two major models
  - Simple unit with three channels and no display
  - Sophisticated model with 99 channels and a 115 character display
  - Special models for specific situations such as for hazardous use
- Range of additional features
  - Vehicle adapters
  - Selection of antennas
  - Hands-free unit
  - Headset use under a helmet for hazardous conditions.

Private Mobile Radio Systems and Applications

Figure 6.1 shows PMR systems of varying sizes and sample models. A small PMR system can serve up to 100 people in one site. It usually needs just one antenna and has one control unit. A medium system can serve up to 1,000 users, also from one single base station. It can be used on site, or for local area use. Examples of medium systems are the Motorola/Storno model 220 system and the Ericsson MRS 4040 model. Large systems can serve up 10,000 users, and usually provide

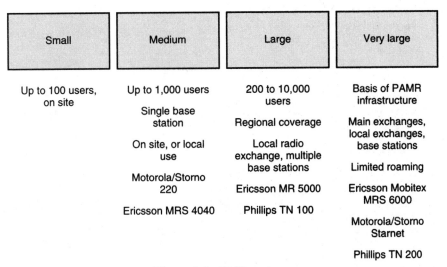

Figure 6.1 PMR systems.

regional coverage. They require multiple base stations. Examples are the Ericsson MRS 5000, and the Phillips TN 100 systems. Very large systems have infrastructures that border on being a PAMR system. They have hierarchical switching structures, and in some cases provide limited handover, a feature that most mobile radio systems do not provide.

The target markets for PMR systems are shown in Figure 6.2 The very small systems are usually applied to taxi companies and other service dispatch types of companies. The larger systems apply to manufacturing, transport, and emergency applications.

The mobile radio buying groups are for example:

- Repair and maintenance staff in
  - Utilities
  - Petrochemical plants
  - High technology industries
- Ambulance drivers, taxi drivers, and couriers
- Site management for
  - Airports
  - Railway stations
  - Construction sites
  - Police and fire officers.

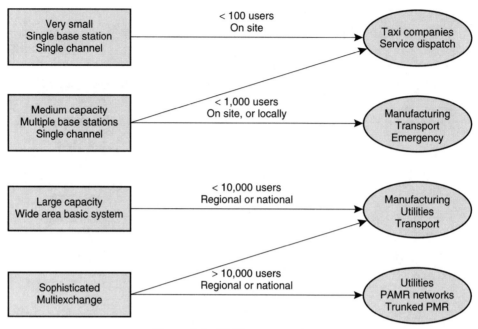

Figure 6.2   PMR target markets.

Applications of PMR, PAMR, and Cellular

Whether to use PMR, PAMR, or cellular depends on the traffic pattern of the organization and a number of other factors. Figure 6.3 can help explain the situation.

If most of the traffic is within the organization and people in the organization seldom talk to people outside the group, then PMR would be the best from a community interest point of view. If

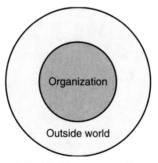

Figure 6.3   Traffic patterns discussion.

people within the group talk often to others within the group as well as to people outside the group, then PAMR would be a better choice. If the people in the group hardly spoke to each other, but spoke to the outside world often, then cellular is the best solution.

Other factors that enter into the decision between PMR and PAMR are akin to the factors that enter into the decision between buying a PBX or using a centrex, namely:

- With a PAMR system, the user does not have to have staff to operate, maintain, and manage the system
- With a PAMR system, the user does not have to acquire additional equipment, install it, and troubleshoot it to enlarge the system; he simply asks the PAMR provider for additional capacity
- With PAMR systems, the user does not have as much control on what exact features the system will have
- With PAMR, the user is not guaranteed the channels at all times
- With PAMR, the user must pay on a per-use basis, and the cost may be larger than owning and operating his own system
- In many countries, there is pressure to use PAMR systems instead of PMR systems, because of the spectral efficiency of PAMR systems.

Mobile Radio Supply Chain

The supply chain for mobile radio is depicted in Figure 6.4. There are two chains, one for PMR, and one for PAMR. At the beginning of the chain are the subsystem manufacturers providing chip sets and other subsystems to the infrastructure suppliers who produce switching equipment and base stations. These are provided to the network operators, who supply the PAMR service providers. The terminals are supplied to the users directly, through dealers, or through the network operators and service providers. PMR systems are put together by PMR distributors who obtain PMR systems from PMR manufacturers and terminals from terminal manufacturers.

Some mobile radio suppliers and the types of systems they supply are shown in Figure 6.5.

A sample PMR system architecture is shown in Figure 6.6. The PMR system uses the PBX network as its backbone network. Dispatch units, supervisors, and network management units are connected to the PMR system via the PBX network.

For example, the Phillips TN 100 system has the following characteristics:

- Nodal architecture, each node contains
  - Switch
  - Processor
  - Network management

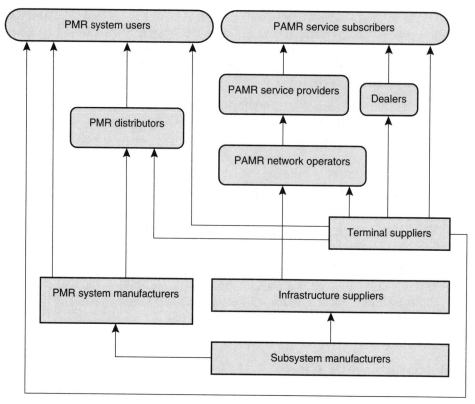

Figure 6.4   Mobile radio supply chain.

- Sites and nodes are linked by leased lines of the PSTN
- Modular growth
- Nodes can be duplicated for redundancy
- Built to the MPT 1327 standard
- Can serve
  - A single site
  - A multinode network serving thousands of users
- Full network monitoring and management
- Group calls
- Emergency message capability

Supplier	PMR systems	PAMR infrastructure	PAMR services
AEG	*	o	o
Alcatel	**	*	o
Ascom	***	o	o
Bosch	***	*	o
Ericsson	**	***	*
Motorola/Storno	****	***	**
Philips/AP	****	***	**

Figure 6.5   Mobile radio suppliers.

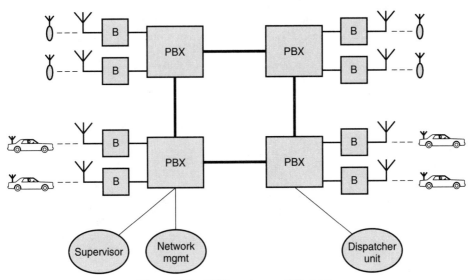

Figure 6.6   PMR system architecture.

- Interconnection to PBXs
- Multiple dispatch capability
- Dynamic channel allocations between sites from a central pool.

Relationship of PMR and PAMR to SMR and ESMR

Mobile radio systems have different names throughout the world. In Europe they are called PMR and PAMR. In the United States they are called Specialized Mobile Radio and Enhanced Mobile Radio. Some of these systems provide voice services; some provide data services. Figure 6.7 plots these systems in a matrix that has voice and data as one axis, and private and public on the other. The DSRR and Tetra standards are superimposed on the figure.

PMR systems have traditionally provided voice services to private groups. PAMR has also provided voice services, but on a shared basis. SMR in the states has also provided predominantly voice services, but also data services to private groups. The term ESMR is new and refers to companies such as Nextel who are acquiring SMR licenses nationwide to put together a network to compete with cellular. They are developing their own proprietary architecture to provide integrated voice and data. The protocol is similar to GSM, but is not GSM.

Digital Short Range Radio is aimed at standardizing PMR, and provides both voice and data. Tetra is aimed at standardizing PAMR, and also provides both voice and data. In fact, it provides both circuit-switched as well as packet-switched data. It is a well-thought through standard that is being proposed for many applications worldwide including groups that have been traditionally served by PMR systems. It remains to be seen whether these groups will feel sufficiently comfort-

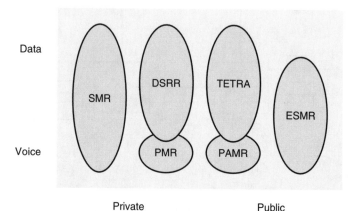

Figure 6.7   Relationship of PMR, PAMR, SMR, ESMR, and the standards.

able with the system to adopt it in place of their private system. One main issue is whether they will be able to get the number of channels they require to handle an emergency or other situation where very high demand can be concentrated in a small geographical area.

Summary

In summary, in this chapter we discussed the applications of Private Mobile Radio and Public Access Mobile Radio and how these two systems relate to cellular; the relationship of PMR and PAMR systems with Specialized Mobile Radio; and Enhance Specialized Mobile Radio systems. We also examined mobile radio technologies for private systems—small, medium, and large—as well as public systems. Finally, we showed where the Digital Short Range Radio standard for PMR and the Tetra standard for PAMR fit in, and the challenges they face.

7 *Conclusions*

In this chapter, we present some of the highlights of the book, and make concluding remarks regarding PCS and related cellular services.

PCS and Cellular Market

In the first chapter of the book, we discussed the market for cellular and related services, namely cordless and PCS. We put these services into perspective by presenting several wireless maps. The first map shown in Figure 7.1 presents the evolution of products and services as well as the standards and spectra for wireless networking activities throughout the world including not just cellular and PCS, but also Wireless LANs and Mobile Data services.

This book has focused on the middle three columns of the figure covering Wireless PBXs, residential and public access, and mobile services. We discussed Wireless LANs and mobile data briefly. Another book entitled *Mobile Data and Wireless LANs* covers those two areas in detail. The picture is complex particularly for the worldwide traveler who would like to have wireless access no matter where he is, and be able to use one simple device as shown in Figure 7.2. It will be some time before we can use a single device to access the network no matter where we happen to be.

We presented the map of data rate and cell size shown in Figure 7.3 that compares the services and analyzes their relationship.

The services are clustered around a curve that starts at the high-data rate, small cell-size corner of the figure and moves to the low-data rate large-cell size corner of the chart. In order to obtain high-data rates for future multimedia applications, we have to evolve to small-cell systems. The first step is to move to small-cell cellular systems like high-tier PCS systems. The next step is to use very small-cell systems like low-tier PCS systems.

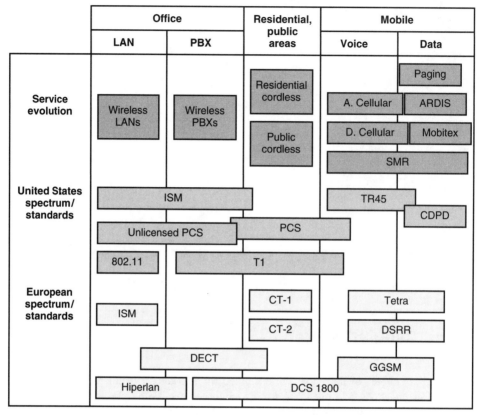

Figure 7.1 Standards and spectrum activities.

We discussed the phases of growth of the cellular and related services market. As shown in Figure 7.4, we see that analog cellular is in the maturation phase, digital cellular is in the robust growth phase, high-tier PCS systems are in the early adopter stage, and low-tier systems are pre–early adopter.

We discussed market forecasts for four major areas of the world: North America, Europe, the Pacific Rim, and the rest of the world. As shown in Figure 7.5, we found that North America starts out last, but garners a roughly equal if not slightly larger share compared with the other regions of the world.

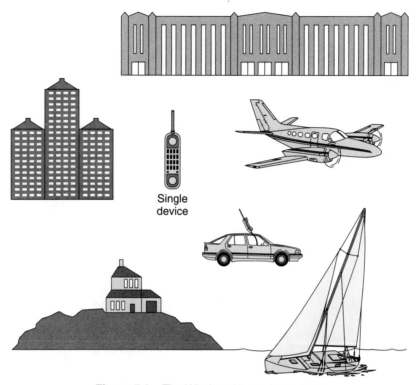

Figure 7.2 The Wireless Networking vision.

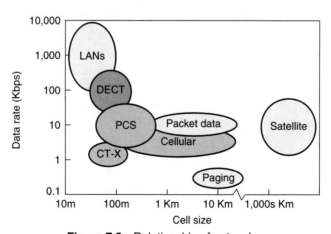

Figure 7.3 Relationship of networks.

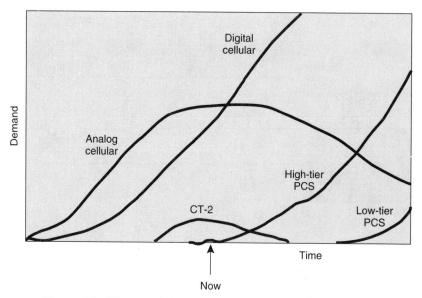

Figure 7.4 The growth patterns of cellular and related services.

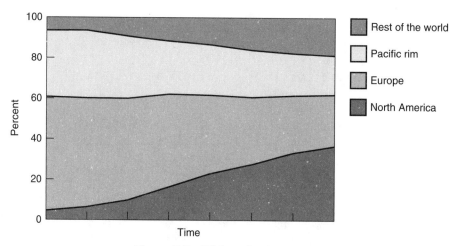

Figure 7.5 PCS market by region.

Propagation and Modulation Techniques

In the second chapter we laid down the theoretical foundation for cellular and related systems. We developed propagation formulas starting from intuitive ideas. We discussed the basic parameters illustrated in Figure 7.6, and their impact on the application of systems such TDMA, CDMA, GSM and DCS to rural and urban areas.

The larger cell systems use higher power as well as lower frequency to achieve the greater range. The small-cell high-density systems use higher frequency bands, and also use smaller power to allow the handsets to have extra long battery life.

We presented the alternative multiplexing techniques illustrated in Figure 7.7, and discussed their merits.

We discussed CDMA and showed how it works as depicted in Figure 7.8.

We described multiple access techniques and compared them including the controversial comparison between TDMA and CDMA. CDMA can theoretically provide greater spectrum efficiency and features such as soft handoff. It is a much more complex system that will take time to work smoothly in large-scale implementations.

Finally, we presented the basics of cellularization principles and showed the choices made by the major digital cellular systems. Figure 7.9 shows an example of using different cell size systems in high-density downtown areas, and larger cell systems in the suburbs.

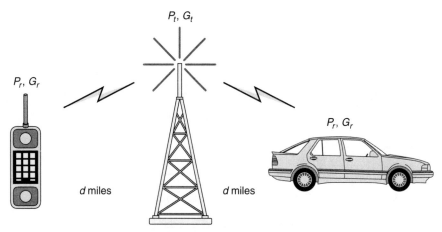

Figure 7.6 Radio propagation parameters.

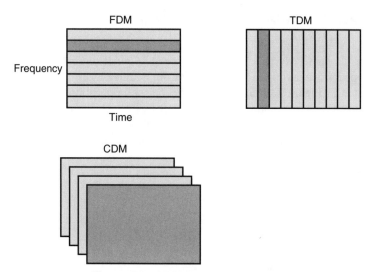

Figure 7.7   Multiplexing techniques.

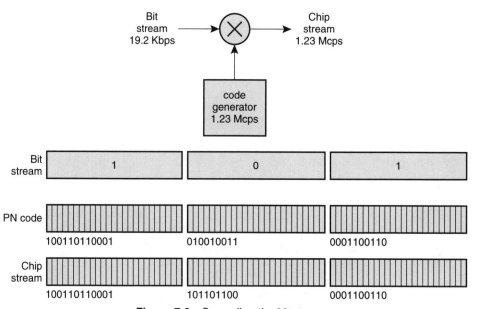

Figure 7.8   Spreading the bit stream.

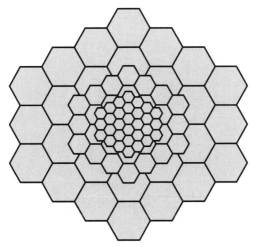

Figure 7.9   Cellular design.

Cellular Technologies

In the third chapter, we presented the major cellular systems in the world, compared them to each other, and to satellite systems. We started with analog cellular systems including AMPS, NMT, and TACS. Then we discussed the four competing digital cellular standards that are compared in Figure 7.10, namely GSM/DCS, PDC, TDMA, and CDMA.

The race is on. GSM has an early lead. Whoever maintains an early lead may be the eventual big winner, because whoever reaches large volumes first can reduce cost first and expand market share even more. The advanced technology of CDMA is working both for and against the system.

Standard	MAC	Carrier BW	Channels/ carrier	Modulation
GSM	FDMA/TDMA	200 KHz	8 (16)	GMSK
IS-54	FDMA/TDMA	30 KHz	3 (6)	π/4 DQPSK
IS-95	CDMA	1.23 MHz	64 (128)	BPSK
PDC	FDMA/TDMA	25 KHz	3 (6)	π/4 DQPSK

Figure 7.10   Digital cellular standards.

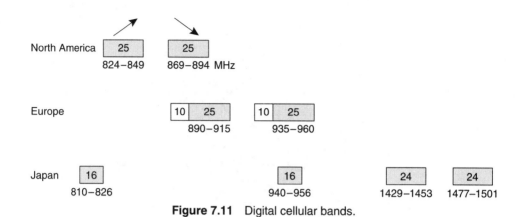

Figure 7.11 Digital cellular bands.

Its complexity is proving a difficult hurdle to overcome in the early implementations, but that very complexity is what may make it a winner in the long term, as it has the potential of providing the most efficient system for future high-density applications. The frequency allocations for digital cellular are shown in Figure 7.11.

Satellite systems fill in the holes for cellular and allow the worldwide traveler to have access in all parts of the world even in the near term as cellular systems achieve greater and greater coverage. The major satellite systems are summarized in Figure 7.12. Several LEO systems are being implemented. Combined Iridium/GSM handsets can provide seamless integration of the satellite and cellular systems. They would use cellular where available and use satellite only when required.

Figure 7.12 Public satellite systems.

GSM/DCS

In the fourth chapter, we began with the objectives of GSM/DCS as stated in the standard. We presented the voice and data features of the system. The voice is based on a 13 Kbps vocoding technique called RELP. Data can be sent up to 9.6 Kbps in Phase 2 of GSM. There are proposals to extend that up to the range of 100 Kbps by combining voice grade channels up to the capacity of one whole carrier. This is a proposal for GSM Phase 2+. Data require data sets to be inserted between the data device and the cellular phone, and a modem or data device to be inserted at the network between the cellular connection and the PSTN.

We presented the functional architecture shown in Figure 7.13, and discussed the open interfaces that allow different manufacturers to implement different parts of the system: for example, phones, base stations, switching centers, and databases. In particular we pointed out that the SIM interface will see more applications than it was originally envisioned to have, for example, roaming to different present services as well as roaming to future third-generation services.

We discussed the signaling structure of GSM and showed how the system works, and how certain features are obtained, specifically, the Short Message feature and the Cell Broadcast service. We presented the frequency and time channelization scheme. We detailed the three parts of security of GSM including the authentication process depicted in Figure 7.14, the data privacy

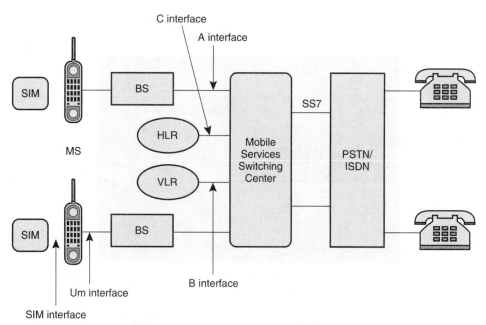

Figure 7.13   GSM Functional architecture.

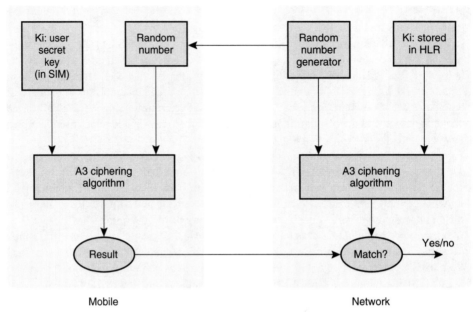

Figure 7.14 Authentication process.

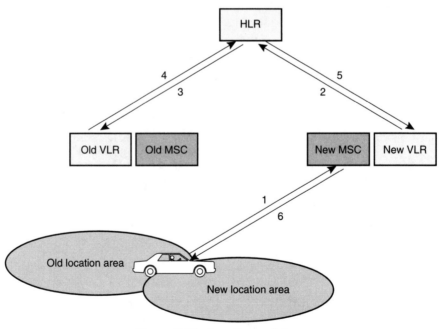

Figure 7.15 Location updating.

process, and the privacy of the user location. The authentication capability of GSM and other digital cellular systems greatly reduces the problem of cellular fraud that is costing the industry billions of dollars and causing great inconvenience to users.

Finally, we showed how mobility is handled as the user moves from one location area served by one MSC to another location area served by another MSC as illustrated in Figure 7.15.

Cordless Telephony and PCS Systems

In the fifth chapter, we discussed cordless telephony and PCS. We started with the roots of cordless telephony in the present widespread analog of cordless phones we all have in our homes. These systems are summarized in Figure 7.16.

There are a great many analog cordless phones in the United States and Japan. These are the market roots for future low-cost PCS systems. We then discussed the digital cordless systems, namely CT-2, CT-2+, DECT, and PHS. These are summarized in Figure 7.17.

Early implementations of CT-2 have served as a vehicle for learning. These early implementations are gradually being replaced by high-tier PCS implementations. DECT and PACS are two of the proposed low-tier PCS standards. DECT has the potential of being a worldwide wireless PBX standard.

Then we looked at PCS in detail. The frequency allocations for it are shown in Figure 7.18.

The PCS bands have been auctioned. The auctioning is a milestone in the Wireless Networking industry. It is reshaping the industry as much as the splitting of the Bell System did, and it seems to be working in the opposite direction. It is leading to a regrouping of the major telecommunications forces in the United States. This trend is likely to spread to other parts of the world, as the temptation of revenue from the auctions becomes irresistible to other governments. The cost of auctioning to the end user is significant. A rough estimate of about 25 percent of the total cost of the service is a result of the cost of auctioning. In essence, auctioning is a tax levied on the users' Wireless Networking.

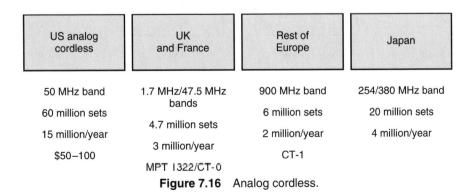

Figure 7.16 Analog cordless.

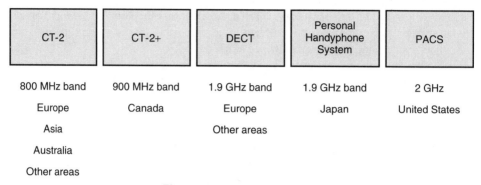

Figure 7.17 Digital cordless.

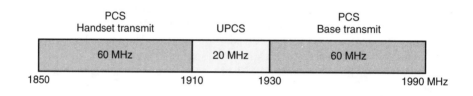

Figure 7.18 PCS spectrum allocations.

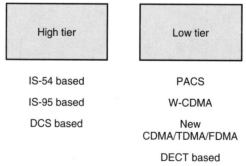

Figure 7.19 The seven PCS standards.

The unlicensed PCS bands are not auctioned at this time; we will see how long this lasts. As with the licensed PCS bands, the UPCS bands have to be cleared before they can be used. The Wireless PBX industry is moving forward expeditiously to clear the isochronous bands. The Wireless LAN industry is not moving ahead as fast, for they claim that the whole band must be cleared nationwide before the first system can use it. No one company is willing to start funding such clearing when the revenues from the service are not yet flowing.

The seven proposed standards for PCS are summarized in Figure 7.19. High-tier systems are now in the early adopter stage of development. They are supplementing cellular systems and serving the additional demand for Wireless Networking by utilizing the higher PCS band allocations. Low-tier systems will come much later, as the demand matures, and price of the service comes down.

Figure 7.20 summarizes the comparison between cordless and cellular systems. Cordless and PCS systems clearly serve islands of high-density users with low-complexity systems. Cellular systems provide ubiquitous coverage with larger cells, lower frequency, and higher power handsets.

Figure 7.21 shows the interaction between wired and wireless loops. In some countries, where the present penetration of wired telephony is extremely low, say below 2 percent, it is viable

	Cordless	**Cellular**
Cell size	Small (50 to 500 m)	Large (0.5 to 30 Km)
Antenna elevation	Low (15 m or less)	High (15 m or more)
Mobility speed	Slow (< 6 Km/hr)	Fast (< 250 Km/hr)
Coverage	Zonal	Ubiquitous
Handset complexity	Low	Moderate
Base complexity	Low	High
Average TX power	2 to 10 mw	100 to 600 mw
Duplexing	TDD	FDD
Coding	32 Kbps ADPCM	8 to 13 Kbps
Error control	CRC	FEC
Multipath mitigation	Antenna diversity	Diversity/equalizer/Rake

Figure 7.20 Comparison of cordless and cellular.

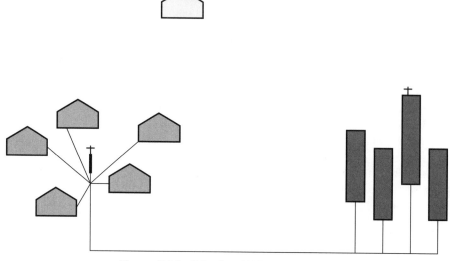

Figure 7.21 Wired and Wireless Loops.

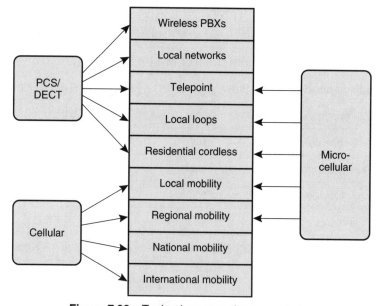

Figure 7.22 Technology mapping to markets.

to use wireless loops to provide access quickly and economically. In countries where the penetration of telephony is significant, it is likely that wireless loops will be installed as a supplement to the wired network. In fact, it is likely that the wired network will provide greater and greater bandwidth through ISDN to meet the need for high bandwidth applications in the home such as internet access, shopping at home, and entertainment.

Figure 7.22 summarizes the applications for cellular, microcellular or high-tier PCS, and PCS systems. The solid lines in the figure indicate that PCS systems are the primary candidate for meeting the needs of Wireless PBXs, local networks, telepoint, local loops, and residential cordless. Cellular meets the needs of mobile users at various levels. Microcellular, or high-tier PCS systems serve the intermediate applications and serve as a bridge between cellular systems and low-tier PCS systems of the future.

The frequency allocations for high-tier and low-tier PCS systems near 2 GHz are compared to the allocations for satellite and future third-generation systems in Figure 7.23. Clearly, the way to greater bandwidth is to move the higher frequencies as the technology allows it cost-effectively.

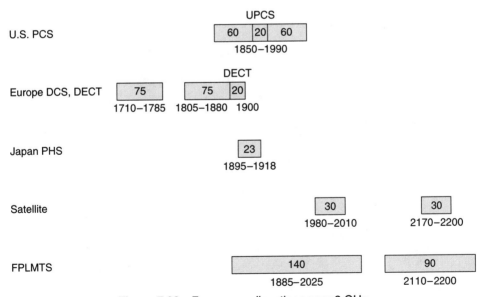

Figure 7.23   Frequency allocations near 2 GHz.

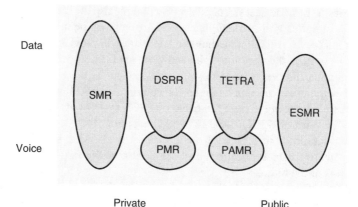

Figure 7.24   Relationship of PMR, PAMR, SMR, ESMR, and the standards.

Mobile Radio

In the sixth chapter we discussed the applications of Private Mobile Radio and Public Access Mobile Radio and how these two systems relate to cellular. We also examined mobile radio technologies for private systems—small, medium, and large—as well as for public systems. The rela-

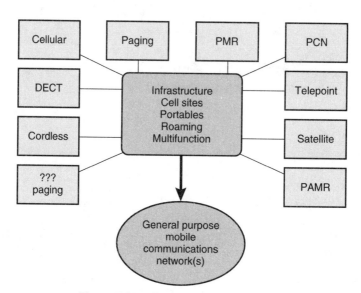

Figure 7.25   Trend towards unification.

tionship of PMR and PAMR systems with Specialized Mobile Radio and Enhance Specialized Mobile Radio systems is illustrated in Figure 7.24.

The Digital Short Range Radio standard is aimed at PMR applications, and the Tetra standard is aimed at PAMR applications. They both provide integrated voice and data capabilities. Tetra is meeting with great interest throughout the world. Its challenge is to meet the needs of specialized groups who are accustomed to having a private network with guaranteed channels.

We have discussed a great many services in this book. It seems that each service is being implemented on its separate network in the early development stages of this industry. How many separate network infrastructures can the market support? The question is likely to be answered over time, as market shares are defined and an actual return on investment becomes clear. Figure 7.25 suggests that some integration of infrastructure may be in order.

As each network is composed of cell sites, switched, and interconnection facilities, we will look for ways of providing the different services, through the software definition of the services, not by separate networks.

Bibliography

Calhoun, G. *Digital Cellular Radio,* Norwood, MA: Artech House, 1988.

ETSI, *European Telecommunication Standard, DECT, ETS 300 175,* parts 1–9 and ETS 300 176.

ETSI, *European Telecommunications Standards Institution,* "Recommendations for GSM 900/DCS 1800," published by ETSI, 06921 Sophia Antipolis, Cedex, France.

Gilhousen, K. S., et al. "On the Capacity of a Cellular DCMA System," *IEEE Trans. on Vehicular Technology,* vol. VT-40, no. 2, May 1992.

Gudmundson, B., et. al. "A Comparison of CDMA and TDMA Systems," *Proc. 42nd IEEE Vehicular Technology Conf.,* Denver, May 1992.

Hodges, M. L. "The GSM Radio Interface," *Br. Telecom Technol. Journal,* vol. 8, no. 1, January 1990.

Lee, W. Y. C. *Mobile Cellular Telecommunications Systems,* New York: McGraw-Hill International, 1989.

Macario, R. *Personal & Mobile Radio Systems*, Peter Peregrimus, Ltd., 1992.

"Mobile Communications Towards the Year 2000," *Proc. of IEE Professional Group E8* (radio communications systems), London, October 17, 1994.

Mouly, M., and Marie-B. Pautet. *The GSM System for Mobile Communications,* France, 1992.

Mulder, R. J. "DECT, a Universal Cordless Access System," *Phillips Telecommunication Review,* vol. 49, no. 3, September 1992.

Ramsdale, P. B., and W. B. Harrold. "Techniques for Cellular Networks Incorporating Microcells," *IEEE Conf. PIMR 92,* Boston, October 1992.

Selected proceedings of the T1 Standards Committee and its subcommittees.

Selected proceedings of the TR45 Standards Committee and its subcommittees.

Steele, R. *Mobile Radio Communications,* London: Pentech Press, 1992.

APPENDIX A

Wireless Networking Applications

Many of us are beginning to depend on mobile computers and wireless modems of various forms and functions. Mobile Data networks and Wireless LANs empower these devices by connecting them to each other and to the information we need wirelessly. When we are in the office, our data communications needs are typically served by a LAN. Outside of the office, we usually rely on public data networks. How will our needs for mobility and wireless connectivity be met in these two environments? In this first Appendix chapter, we discuss who will be mobile and also include examples of vertical and horizontal applications of Wireless Networking. Wireless Networking can be considered to be part of Mobile Computing as shown in Figure A.1.

At the top layer of the Mobile Computing chart are vertical and horizontal applications. Vertical applications are those that apply to a functional part of an industry such as field sales and field service, or to a specific market segment, notably banking or health care.

The next layer is the mobile operating systems layer. This layer provides tools for application programmers to access different mobile devices and different Wireless Networks. These tools make the job of the application programmers much easier, for they do not have to be concerned with the details and complexities of underlying networks or on how these networks or their interfaces change over time. This is a critical layer that is key to the rapid growth of Wireless Networking and the desired proliferation of compelling applications that companies can utilize to provide their customers with added value.

The next level is the device level. These are all the mobile devices we carry with us including notebook computers, Personal Digital Assistants, cellular phones, Personal Communicators, and combination devices that have several functions. Combination devices are beginning to emerge. It is delightful to watch the results of people's imagination as they produce just the right combination of features for the right market segment. Appendix A provides details concerning the Mobile Computing device level and the mobile operating system level.

Carrying this traffic are Wireless Networks, both wide area and local area. Wireless Networks are the main subject of this book. The area of Wireless Wide Area Networks is also called "Mobile Data," which encompasses packet networks such as RAM/Mobitex and ARDIS/Modacom, paging networks, data over cellular—both analog and digital—and data over satellite chan

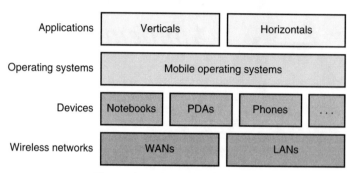

Figure A.1 Mobile Computing.

nels. Wireless LANs provide much higher data rates than Mobile Data networks but are confined to an office building or campus.

In this appendix, we discuss the applications of Wireless Networking, in particular:

- Vertical and horizontal applications of Wireless Networking
- Market dynamics
- Vertical applications examples
- Challenges
- Case studies
- Applications/technology matrix
- Horizontal applications examples
- Positioning of Wireless Networking relative to wired networks

We are now focusing on the top level of the Mobile Computing chart as highlighted in Figure A.1.

Vertical and Horizontal Applications of Wireless Networking

The pie chart in Figure A.2 shows that by the year 2005 almost half of the people using Mobile Computing will be performing mobile office applications. About a quarter of the people are using it for personal communications. The rest are in vertical applications such as field sales, field service, and transportation.

In the field sales application, the salesperson arrives at the customer's location armed with his mobile computer. He is able to perform the following functions while at the customer site; at the same time, he is connected to servers back at his home office, or to any database he needs to perform his job:

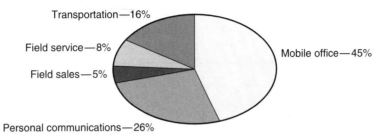

Figure A.2 Mobile Computing applications market segments.

- Sales quotation
- Inventory check
- Order entry
- Credit authorization
- Invoicing.

The field service engineer could be traveling through his territory in a company van or flying around the country to his accounts. The functions that are possible with this vertical application are:

- Obtaining a maintenance history of the item requiring service
- Performing complex diagnostics that require access to databases and applications at other locations
- Checking parts inventory if required
- Updating the maintenance database after the service is done
- Invoicing for the job
- Real time dispatching of the field engineer.

Perhaps the oldest Wireless Networking applications area is transportation. Wireless Networking has been used in this area for many years to communicate with fleets of trucks, taxis, parcel delivery vans, and so on. The different kinds of transportation applications are endless. The functions performed include:

- Automatic location of the vehicle
- Dispatching of the vehicle to the next job
- Routing the vehicle if required
- Capturing data from the vehicle.

Horizontal applications, which are envisioned to account for the majority of the market in a few years are illustrated in Figure A.3. These horizontal applications are essentially what we would be doing if we were connected to a wire in the wall. With wireless, we are able to perform them

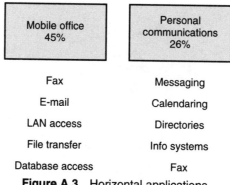

Figure A.3   Horizontal applications.

wherever we are, as long as we are in range of the backbone networks that contain the information we need. It is interesting to keep in mind that when we carry the mobile devices with us, we are likely to use them for business as well as for personal use. Therefore, in designing them we have to remember that a person may, for example, choose to have a single calendar that contains both his business appointments as well as his personal appointments. He may choose to have single or multiple directories—one for his business associates and one for his family and friends.

Market Dynamics

In this section, we discuss the dynamics of the market with regard to readiness for volume shipments along with consideration of vertical and horizontal applications. We believe that the Wireless Networking market is on the brink of a new phase, as shown in Figure A.4. It is complet-

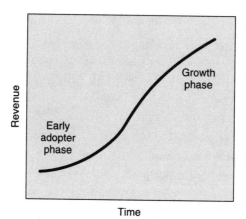

Figure A.4   Phases of the Wireless Networking Market.

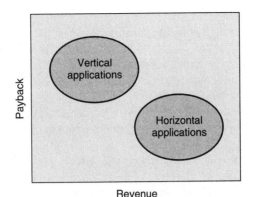

Figure A.5   Vertical and horizontal market dynamics.

ing the phase of the early adopters and is ready for large growth. To achieve this we will need large suppliers who provide the volume required and a spectrum of full services.

Figure A.5 shows the market dynamics for vertical applications and for horizontal applications. Initial revenue potential is in vertical markets. Payback of the investment in Mobile Computing is easy to quantify for vertical applications where the increase in productivity is directly identifiable.

Horizontal applications require prices to drop significantly. The payback is not as easy to quantify, but the volume of users is much larger.

Vertical Market Examples

The applications of Wireless Networking are increasing every day. In this section, we present the following sample applications:

- Airlines
- Police
- Emergency
- Hospitals
- Maintenance
- Retail stores
- Stock exchanges.

Today, the use of Wireless Networking is obvious in the operation of airports. We see airport personnel with various forms of mobile radio handsets communicating with each other and with the head office. We are beginning to see the use of these portable devices in assisting passengers in the check-in process. While standing in line, an attendant may ask you if you have any baggage to check-in. If you don't, he or she can check you in on the spot. These are the very tip of the iceberg of the potential of Wireless Networking in the airline industry. In the future, we should be able to use smart cards for check-in automatically, and our baggage can be animated with these same smart cards to route it to its correct destination.

The insurance example depicted in Figure A.6 is a classical field sales application. The salesperson can use a mobile computer to provide accurate quotes and obtain approval of the underwriters in real time.

In the future, we can provide an application that will be able to use artificial intelligence and be connected to the home office to determine what additional products this customer would benefit from. An interactive presentation would be available to show the customer the products and their benefits to his or her specific situation.

Police and emergency services are classical applications of Wireless Networking and are a ripe potential for Mobile Computing. As we obtain greater bandwidth, we can provide more complete information on suspects including their pictures, or sketches of them, their last known location, whether or not they are armed, and the information is up to the minute.

In the case of emergency services such as ambulances, the availability of greater bandwidth enables emergency personnel to communicate more accurately to acquire complete information on the status of the patient and obtain more detailed instructions for the start of treatment on the way to the hospital. This is pictured in Fig A.7. In the ambulance, emergency personnel are able to check on the patient, and start the diagnostics and treatment process with the help of an emergency room doctor who is in the hospital and connected in real time with the ambulance. Multimedia transfers can relay the patient's vital signs and even pictures of the injury to the attending physician.

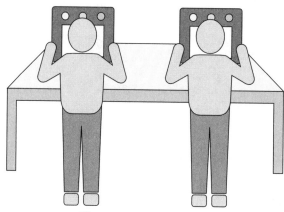

Figure A.6 Field sales.

Figure A.7 Emergency services.

At the hospital, Wireless Networking can provide more accurate and up-to-date information to doctors and nurses.

Nurses and doctors can:

- Access patient records
- Use diagnostic databases
- Preview surgery to patient
- Order medication.

Another health care example (pictured in Fig A.8) that can benefit from Wireless Networking is the mobile roving doctor. This is an idea that is being experimented with in Europe. At night and on weekends, doctors ride in vans that are dispatched to patients who need care. When the doctor is dispatched to the next patient, that patient's record is downloaded to the vehicle. After the doctor attends to the patient, he enters his report directly into the database back at the home office or hospital, and indicates that he is now free for the next call.

For a fleet of vehicles, time wasted in the shop is a critical cost factor. Today, when the operator detects a problem with the vehicle, he must schedule time in the shop to perform diagnostics and repair. In the future, sensors and smart applications in the vehicles can continuously monitor vehicle performance, perform diagnostics, and when needed contact the nearest repair center wirelessly to schedule a service appointment.

For fixed machines, today, maintenance engineers perform their duty using hand-held Mobile Computing devices. They essentially tour their territory to check the machines they are as-

Figure A.8 Health care vertical application.

signed to maintain. In the future, the fixed equipment can have sensors that call the maintenance engineer when service is required.

Application of Wireless Networking in the retail industry is illustrated by the following example. You enter your favorite department store; the shopping cart has a video display. As you walk through the store, specials in that area of the store are flashed before you. If you are looking for a specific item, you can ask the device and it shows you where it is and how to get there.

During peak shopping seasons, the store may want to add check-out counters or have special counters outdoors. Mobile Computing allows this with ease and with no bother with special wiring.

In larger stores, sales personnel are already using Mobile Computing to help customers spend their money more efficiently! Sales personnel are able to provide up-to-date information on products, fill the order, and perform the transactions on the spot. Walmart stores are using more than 19,000 portable computers, 1,800 base stations, 60 wireless repeaters, and more than 16,000 portable printers. Retail store customized service is pictured in Figure A.9.

A new chain of superstores called the Incredible Universe is also equipping their personnel with wireless terminals. The Incredible Universe is a combination of an electronics store, a computer store, an appliance store, an office products store, a record shop, a photography shop, and a home improvement store. It also has restaurants and day care! The whole family goes there for the afternoon and leaves with filled trunks and filled credit-card balances. Salespeople in the Incredible Universe use Wireless Networking to:

- Check inventory
- Order equipment to be ready at checkout
- Determine equipment requirements.

The stock exchanges are perhaps the most exciting applications of Mobile Computing as pictured in Figure A.10. There is no question that time can be saved and that greater accuracy can be achieved on the stock exchange trading floor. Deals are made and broken in seconds. With Wireless Networking, traders can do trades wherever they are rather than having to run to hard-wired terminals.

Figure A.9   Retail store customized service.

A very interesting application of Wireless Networking is in casinos application. If one examines how a casino operates, one would discover that the gaming tables are arranged in circles or ovals. Looking closely, you would notice that each circle or oval of tables is run by a supervisor. This person is responsible for the profitability of the group of tables. He is called the pit boss, where the "pit" is the group of tables he is responsible for. A good pit boss gets to know the high rollers who frequent the casino. He gets to know their likes and dislikes, the kind of drinks they like, the kind of games they like, and their credit limit. Casinos lend hundreds of millions of dollars annually to their high rollers. Most of these loans are on paper chits that are prone to error.

Suppose the pit boss were equipped with a mobile computer, preferably an unobtrusive PDA that is wirelessly connected to various databases. On this PDA, the pit boss would be able to access the server containing all the specific information about his high rollers including all their likes and dislikes as well as how much money they owe the casino. Such an application has been experimented with and forms of it are being developed.

Hotel check-in can be a frustrating experience, especially in peak times, when one arrives at the hotel after a long tiring journey only to have to wait in another line. The check-in could take place at an earlier point in the journey, for example, in the courtesy bus from the airport. With Wireless Networking that is possible.

Taxicabs have been using Wireless Networking for a long time. They have used voice until relatively recently, when data terminals have been introduced throughout the world in taxis. However, voice is still retained in most cases for the time being. The data terminal allows the taxi to be

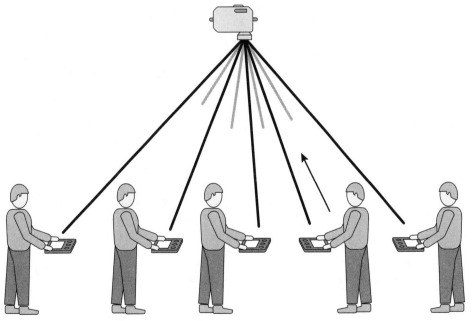

Figure A.10   The stock exchange application.

dispatched to the next customer accurately and securely. A problem with voice dispatching is that a rogue cab can intercept the voice dispatch and beat the authorized cab to the waiting customer.

Data terminals are not yet used exclusively, because they do not have all the features required to operate the cab. For example, if a cabdriver is lost or does not know the location of a specific point, he can ask the dispatcher. At this time, the terminals in cabs do not have this capability. It is hard to tell if voice will disappear from cabs in the future. There is an interesting possibility of putting a public call from the cellular phone in the cab. The customer can then make a public phone call from the cellular phone in the cab. The cost of the call could be automatically added to the fare.

Rental car agencies are one of the most advanced users of Wireless Networking to date. In some airports, the process is very streamlined. When the customer arrives at the airport and has a special preferred status, he boards the rental car bus and gives the driver his rental car card. The driver takes him to an express counter where the contract is ready, and his rental car is nearby. There could be one more step eliminated: The bus driver could take the customer directly to his car, and the contract could be electronic. Upon return, the customer drives the rental car into the rental car lot, a person greets him there with a wireless terminal and checks him in, and prints out a receipt on the spot. This is done today, but the terminals and portable printers that the rental car employees have to carry are a bit heavy and cumbersome.

Truck and train exchange yards are classical users of Wireless Networking. We can think of these yards as a giant packet switch where truck tractors or train cars are switched from one train or one truck to another. Each car or truck has certain goods in it that are destined to a particular place. The address of the container is similar to the header of a packet in a packet switch. The yard is analogous to a Packet Assembly/Disassembly function. Wireless Networking plays a critical role in this classical transportation application.

As we can see, Wireless Networking applications abound, and new ones are developing every day. Wireless Networking is the kind of technology we do not know exactly how to use until we have it. Probably 50 percent of the applications we will have in five years are not envisioned today.

Challenges

The following are excerpts from interviews with MIS managers of major firms that are contemplating using Wireless Networking. These challenges are real. Solutions to them are at hand. The fact that they are highlighted at this time is appropriate to ensure that adequate attention is focused on them early. The major challenges that face Wireless Networking fall in the following areas:

- Security
- Bandwidth
- Software applications
- Safety.

Lehman Brothers is a brokerage house with tens of millions of trades per day. They estimate that using Wireless Networking can reduce the trade execution time from 90 seconds on the average to less than 10 seconds on the average, a huge improvement. Why do they not use Wireless Networking? The major concern in security is depicted in Figure A.11. Can they be sure that an intruder will not be able to enter a bogus transaction and transfer millions of shares of stock to an unauthorized account?

The security issue can be thought of in three areas:

- User authentication for network access
- Data privacy
- Privacy of the location of the user.

First, is the authentication issue. Authentication insures that the right people do get on the network, and unauthorized people do not. Currently, cellular fraud is a huge expense to the industry and a great inconvenience to the users. Second, is the privacy of the data. Privacy is obtained by encryption of the data or the voice. Encryption can use private or public keys. We discuss these options in later chapters. Third, due to the cellular nature of Wireless Networking, the user can be roughly located, because the network knows which cell he is in. The famous car chase in the O. J. Simpson case was started by locating the suspect. His location was found, because he made a cellular call. The police were able to trace the call to the cell and find him there. This is similar to call tracing in the wired telephone network today. The information is known in the network but is kept private except from government agencies such as the Police.

Security of Wireless Networks is a visible issue. Because it is so visible, much attention is focused on it, and solutions are provided. For this reason, wireless networks are likely to be more secure than wired networks in the end.

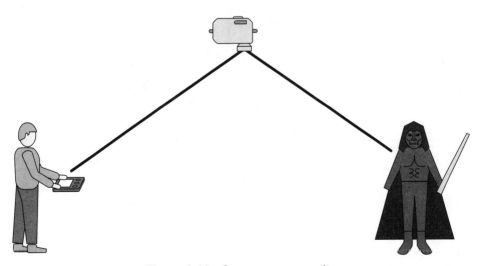

Figure A.11   Concern over security.

Another concern of Lehman Brothers is whether Wireless Networking has sufficient bandwidth to handle its application. Why would there be concern over bandwidth in a stock-trading application? Each transaction is a very small amount of data. Figure A.12 suggests the reason.

In the stock market when something important happens, everyone wants to access the network literally at the same time. Even though each transaction is a very small amount of data, the system has to be able to handle almost all the terminals at the same time. Moreover, the access mechanism has to be extremely fair, and the first users requesting service must be the first served. We discuss the implications on the MAC layer from this simple requirement in a later chapter.

Citibank would like to use Wireless Networking but feels that at this time even though hardware is coming along, the right application software is still in the embryonic stage. Many people from other industries would agree that software applications are probably the one biggest reason why Wireless Networking data implementations have lagged behind voice implementations.

Avon has a huge number of salespeople. They would benefit tremendously from Wireless Networking, but Avon is concerned about the safety of the salespeople, and the possible health problem that may be associated with the radiation emanating from the Wireless Networking devices. Wireless Networking has been with us for many years. We do have safety standards in place, and there have not been many cases that have been highlighted in the past regarding the safety of these devices. What is new that is causing added concern?

First, there are many more Wireless Networking devices today than there were ten years ago, and in another ten years the number will be many-fold more. Second, we are holding the devices closer to our bodies, and in particular, closer to our heads as shown in Figure A.13.

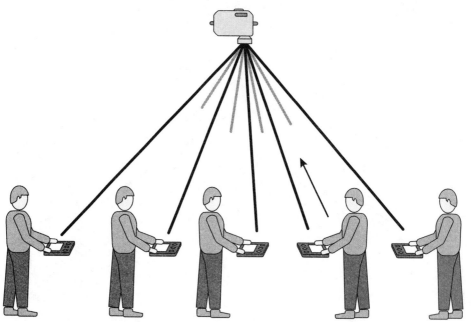

Figure A.12   Concern over sufficient bandwidth in the stock trading application.

Figure A.13   Safety concern over Wireless Networking.

The modulation is digital, and there is some thought that digital modulation can cause more damage to biological tissues than analog modulation. The power levels of today's devices are less than those that were used in the past. In the future, the power levels are envisioned to be even lower. For example, today's cellular phones radiate in the range of 1 watt. Future PCS phones radiate an average on the order of 10 milliwatts.

With the added concern about the safety of Wireless Networking, more research is being done. It is good that the issues are being brought before the public eye, so that funds are made available to pursue the required research. Some of the current organizations and standards for safety in Wireless Networking field are:

- IEEE SCC 28—Standards Coordinations Committee 28
- IEEE COMAR—Scientific Advisory Board
- EPA—Environmental Protection Agency
- FDA—Food and Drug Administration.

Case Studies

In this section, we briefly discuss the following case studies:

- ADP—Automatic Data Processing
- British Airways
- Hewlett Packard in the United Kingdom
- South Dakota University
- Integrated Device Technology
- Revenue Canada.

Automatic Data Processing maintains an auto repair parts database. The database includes all the parts of many automobiles, where to obtain them, how much they cost, and how much labor is involved in replacing the parts. The database is used to provide estimates of repairs of cars after an accident. Due to the high cost of auto repair, the database also includes where to obtain used parts from junkyards and how much they cost. As one can imagine, the used car parts inventory is a very volatile database. When a customer goes into the shop to obtain an estimate for repair, the estimator inspects the car using a mobile computer that is connected to the database by a Mobile Data radio. The estimator is able to pull up a diagram of the car and model. He simply points to the parts that need replacing. When he is finished, an accurate estimate is obtained using not only new parts but possible used parts as well.

British Airways uses Wireless Networking extensively at both Heathrow airport, which is probably the busiest airport in the world, and Gatwick airport, closer in to town. Currently, British Airways uses a Private Mobile Radio system to carry out its operations. It is now considering using a Public Access Mobile Radio system. The functions performed started out traditionally with the myriad of walkie talkies that abound in airports. Now, more and more data terminals are used. Passengers with no baggage to check in are checked in as they wait in the queue. Aircraft final check-out is done by mobile engineers equipped with hand-held wireless devices before handing aircraft over to the pilot. In the future, cabin staff can use hand-held devices to access customer databases and be able to serve frequent flyers with special attention. Currently, there are approximately 1,500 users of Wireless Networking at Heathrow Airport, and 500 Wireless Networking users at Gatwick Airport. The number of communications is about 9,000 over a 10-hour peak period.

Hewlett Packard in the United Kingdom uses Wireless Networking for service engineering. The service engineers are routed to their calls via wireless dispatch. They use the wireless devices to access customer data when they are on the customer site. They service the machines that need repair and enter the service completion information in the remote database while on the customer site.

South Dakota University has a server and network in the basement of one of the campus buildings. The offices that need access to the server and the network are on the first and higher floors. The floors and walls are filled with asbestos. To avoid the hazard of working with asbestos, South Dakota University elected a Wireless Local Area Network solution to provide the needed connectivity without having to run new wiring in the walls or floors.

Integrated Device Technology, a chip maker in Silicon Valley, had a simple requirement to provide the receptionist with access to a database containing the directory of the company. The reception area had high ceilings and a marble floor. To avoid a costly installation of wire, Integrated Device Technology used a Wireless LAN solution to provide the needed connectivity. In the future, they need to provide access to salespeople who come to the home office from time to time. At present, the salespeople have to queue up at wired terminals to perform their functions. In the future, they will be equipped with wireless access, so that if they are in the vicinity of the access point, they can access the information they need.

Revenue Canada is a tax collection agency that has hundreds of branch offices that are geographically dispersed. In order to avoid having to send networking technicians to the remote sites to set up the networks there, Revenue Canada came up with an innovative solution. They bought the personal computers at the headquarters site, ordered wireless LAN devices for them, and set them up at the home office. They then put the computers back in the boxes and shipped them out to the remote offices. At the remote offices, nontechnical staff could take the computers out of the box, plug them in for power, and they were LAN ready. Since the LAN was wireless, it did not require any special connections or debugging by a network technician. Revenue Canada has hundreds of remote offices scattered throughout Canada, so this represented a significant savings over having to send network technicians to each site to set up a wired LAN. This kind of company topology is typical of many companies that have one or more headquarters locations and many more branch locations.

Applications/technology Matrix

In this section, we present an application/technology matrix that shows the technology that best fits certain applications. The matrix is shown in Figure A.14. The applications are shown for the private sector and for the public sector. In the private sector, we have applications such as ser-

Sector	Application	Technology			
		Cellular	Paging	Mobile Data	WLANs
Private (corporate)	Service engineering	★ ★	★	★ ★	★
	Order entry	★ ★	○	★ ★	★
	Vehicle routing	★ ★	○	★ ★	★ ★ ★
	Incident control	★ ★	○	★ ★	★ ★ ★
Public network services	Facsimile	★ ★ ★	○	★	○
	Text messaging	★ ★	★ ★ ★	★ ★ ★	★ ★ ★
	Info services • News • Market • Financial	★ ★ ★	★ ★ ★ ★ ★ ★	★ ★ ★	○ ○ ○
	Location tracking	★	○	○	○
	Traffic alerts	★	★ ★ ★	★ ★	○

Figure A.14   Application/Technology matrix.

vice engineering, order entry, vehicle routing, and incident control. The technologies include cellular, paging, mobile data, and Wireless LANs. The number of stars indicate the degree of applicability of the technology to the applications.

The applications in the public network sector include facsimile transmission, text messaging, and various information services, including news services and vertical information services, such as market data or financial data. Again, the number of stars indicate the degree of applicability of the technology to the application.

Horizontal Applications Examples

In this section, we first discuss near-term horizontal applications, and then the broader horizontal applications that will account for the majority of Wireless Networking revenues in the future.

Examples of near-term horizontal applications abound. One example is any sort of dynamic work environments—a temporary work site, a trade show, or a conference. Another application difficult to wire is in the areas of many old buildings in established office complexes. An additional application is for new employees who need immediate service. One way to serve new employees immediately is to provide them with a wireless terminal while the wiring is installed for their new location.

Examples of broad-based horizontal applications that will be found everywhere include essentially all the functions we do today, but are forced to be connected to the wall to do them. For example, let us consider a meeting that uses Wireless Networking as depicted in Figure A.15. This meeting could be in the office, or it could be a group of individuals from different companies attending a meeting in a hotel or business center. All the activities that require paper or transparencies or slides can be done wirelessly without hard copies. This includes passing private notes. In

Figure A.15   Wireless meeting.

addition, if a person is unable to physically attend the meeting, they can still attend it electronically. And if a person needs to attend another meeting, he can attend it electronically at the same time he is attending this meeting.

Eventually, we will be able to do most of the functions we do today without having to be tethered to a wire as illustrated in Figure A.16.

Another pervasive horizontal application is the wireless traveler. No longer having to depend on the big computer at work, a person can do useful work in the countless hours spent in airports, airplanes, hotel rooms, and so forth. If connectivity to the home office or to any other service is needed, it is only a wireless modem away.

An area that has huge potential for the consumer market is interactive TV. The wireless portion of this application is a sophisticated remote control that controls a TV set top box that is more like a simple personal computer. With the new remote control, we are able to navigate through hundreds of cable channels, order movies on demand, participate in interactive games, order merchandise, obtain educational programs, or just about any kind of information that other people are willing to publish on the Internet.

Interactive TV also has the potential of transforming politics as we know it. The power of the electronic town meetings is not yet tapped. Politicians will be able to put referendums to the people in real time and obtain the answers instantaneously.

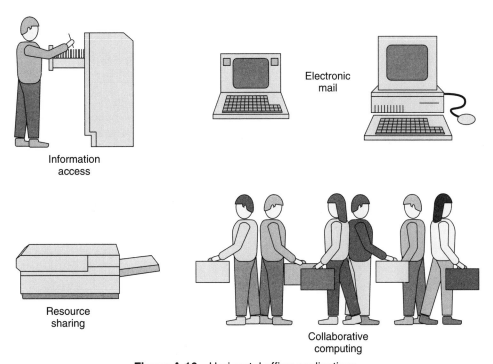

Figure A.16 Horizontal office applications.

	Today	Future
Mobile Data	10 Kbps	100 Kbps
Wireless LANs	1 Mbps	10 Mbps

Figure A.17   Wireless data capabilities.

	Today	Future
Wired Data	100 Kbps	>1 Mbps
Wired LANs	10 Mbps	>100 Mbps

Figure A.18   Wired data capabilities.

Positioning of Wireless Networking Relative to Wired Networks

With the plethora of applications for Wireless Networking that we have today and are sure to see in the future, what will happen to wired networks? Will Wireless Networks replace wired networks all together? To answer this question, let us look at the bandwidth available to wired networks and to Wireless Networks today and in the future. Figures. A.17 and A.18 show some estimates.

Wired networks always have an edge over Wireless Networks in the amount of bandwidth they can offer. Wireless Networks are great for most needs, but we will always want the much larger bandwidth of wired networks for future high-bandwidth multimedia applications. So the position of Wireless Networks relative to wired networks can be summarized as follows:

Not a replacement to wired networks

. . . but an extension to wired networks.

Summary

In summary, in this appendix we focused on the application layer of the Mobile Computing chart. We started by discussing vertical and horizontal applications, in general, showing that the dynamics of the market indicate that vertical applications have the greatest potential for early profits and that they are more easily justified by their users; whereas horizontal applications garner the majority of the revenues in the future but must be priced much lower to appeal to the mass market, both professional and consumer. We presented several vertical market examples including airlines, police, emergency, hospitals, maintenance, retail stores, and stock exchanges. This is but a small sample of what promises to be an expansive industry with applications five years from now that we have not imagined today.

Next, we addressed the major challenges facing the Wireless Networking industry, namely, security, bandwidth, software applications, and safety. We discussed these concerns via results of specific interviews with prospective users of Wireless Networking. Then, we provided several early case studies of users of the technology. The case studies illustrated applications for Mobile Data services and for Wireless LAN products.

Next, we presented an applications/technology matrix showing the private sector applications, the public sector applications, and which of the Wireless Networking technologies applied best. Next, we discussed horizontal applications, starting with early horizontal applications, followed by what will be pervasive horizontal applications that we will all use. Finally, we discussed the position of Wireless Networking relative to wired networks and argued that Wireless Networking is a great adjunct to wired networks that will serve the majority of our needs, but when it comes to high-bandwidth multimedia applications, the wired network remains king.

B Mobile Computing Devices and Operating Systems

In this appendix, we focus on the device level and the operating system level of the Mobile Computing chart shown in Figure B.1. In particular, we cover:

- Mobile computing devices
- Pocketable computing devices
- Underlying technologies
- Mobile operating systems
- Market forecasts.

Mobile Computing Devices

We can think of mobile devices as falling into the categories shown in Figure B.2. Fixed devices are included in Figure B.2 to emphasize that they are very much a part of the picture, as they provide connectivity to the backbone networks and to the servers that hold much of the information we need. The largest mobile computing devices are what can be referred to as carriables—including notebook computers and pen computers. They are of a size that would fit in a briefcase. Though they are easily carried around in an office or on business trips, most people would not carry them much of the time.

The next category includes PDAs, Information Appliances, Personal Communicators, cellular phones, PCS phones, and future navigators of various kinds. They could provide media of several types starting with voice and data and eventually evolving to provide video. Their size is small enough so that they can be put in a pocket or a pocketbook without unduly weighing down the user. A person may take a pocketable with them to dinner; moreover, some people may carry a pocketable with them often or most of the time. A pocketable could include a person's directories and calendar among other items of frequent use.

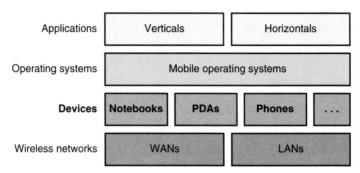

Figure B.1 Mobile Computing.

Wearables are the next category. This category includes smart badges, watch-size pagers, watch-size phones, and other extremely light devices that are smaller than today's pagers. Some envision ring-size devices performing very simple functions. The Star Trek communicator falls into this category! In the last chapter of the book we will discuss future technologies where this category of mobile computing devices is referred to as Tabs.

Another way of looking at mobile computing devices is in perspective relative to fixed devices of different sizes as shown in Figure B.3. At the bottom of the figure are mainframes. Their number is the smallest, but their cost is the highest. Next we have minicomputers, workstations, and desktop PCs, followed by notebook computers and pen-based computers. Finally, at the top we have pocketables and wearables of different kinds. The potential volume of the devices increases as we move upwards in the diagram. Generally, the device cost drops as we move upwards in the diagram. The devices that benefit from mobility are the ones in the top three layers that includes carriables, pocketables, and wearables.

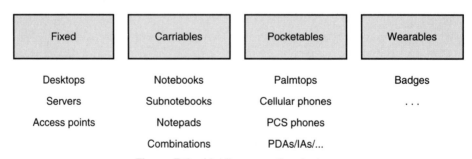

Figure B.2 Mobile computing devices.

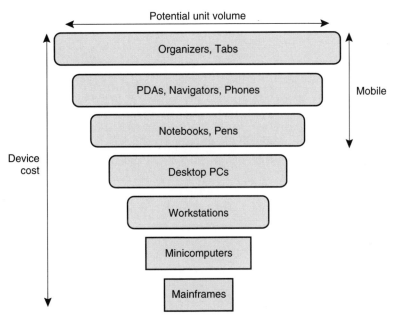

Figure B.3 Computing device cost, potential volume, and mobility.

Pocketable Computing Devices

Let us focus for a moment on the pocketable category. The most common names for these devices are:

- Personal digital assistants
- Information appliances
- Personal communicators.

At first these names may seem whimsical. When considered at a deeper level, they reflect the culture of the part of the industry that coined the term. For example, the term PDA was coined by Apple Computer, and was given to the Newton device that some would say launched the PDA market, albeit too early and with little initial acceptance. What is a PDA? It is a computer that is very simple to use. After much practice, one can write on it with a pen. Its user interface is very simple for a computer, but it is still a computer.

What is a Personal Communicator? This term was coined by AT&T and others who have a culture in the telephony industry. A Personal Communicator is a phone that does a lot more: for example, calendaring, directories, and note taking. Its user interface begins as that of a phone that a five-year-old can operate and goes from there. It is likely to have a wholly different paradigm than a PDA.

What is an Information Appliance? That term is coined by Hewlett Packard. The first pocketable products that HP introduced are the LX series of devices. They look like a calculator for they have buttons like a calculator. In fact, they have the same buttons as the very first calculator that HP produced over 30 years ago, the HP 45. The buttons felt good then, and they still feel good now! It is interesting to note that when the HP 45 first came out, it cost about $400 and was basically a four-function calculator; now we can obtain it for less than $10. The LX series of devices are a full MSDOS machine with 1 Mbyte or more of RAM and start at $400. What is an Information Appliance and how does it differ from a Personal Digital Assistant or a Personal Communicator? An Information Appliance comes with the HP heritage. That heritage is changing, but starts out as a computing device. In fact, the LX series typically comes with a spreadsheet in ROM.

What can pocketable devices do? They:

- Capture information
- Organize information
- Communicate information.

They are built for:

- In-the-field mobile workers

- On-the-go managers

- Mass market consumers.

What do they cost? They vary over a large range all the way from under $100 to over $2,000. Who will be able to buy each kind? Vertical application users can typically afford the most expensive devices, for they can justify the cost of the device more easily. The benefit can be quantified into added functionality in their jobs or operations. For example, a package delivery service is able to justify a pocketable device, because it provides added competitive features that are important to the end user. Notifying the sender of a parcel that the parcel has just been delivered and signed for by the recipient is an example.

The next category of user is the on-the-go manager. To be attractive to the on-the-go manager, the cost needs to be below $1,000. On-the-go managers are the people who spend much of the time away from their desks. They benefit from having critical information with them at their fingertips. Their applications are more horizontal such as in electronic mail, and thus are harder to justify a large expense for them.

Next, we have the general consumer, and there are at least two or three subcategories of consumers. To attract them, the cost needs to be in the $100 range. Below $100 the market can expand significantly to include younger consumers.

Underlying Technologies

To understand the structure of mobile computing devices and how their power will grow with time, we need to look inside one of them as illustrated in Figure B.4. The basic components are: processors, different kinds of memory, and a battery power system. These components are tied together by buses. In addition, with multimedia we are seeing more and more Digital Signal Processing chips. Add-on devices are conforming to the Personal Computer Memory Card Industry Association form factor and are called PCMCIA cards or simply PC cards. Let us now address each of these areas in turn.

Faster processors provide better mobile applications. Mobile devices need the fast processing capability of the newest processors, but they also require small size, cool running, and low cost. The newest fast processors tend to run at a high temperature, and they consume a lot of power. These factors are being addressed and will be solved in the near future. The fast processors are also too expensive for most mobile devices. Mobile devices are not large, expensive workstations where the cost of the processor is a small percentage of the total cost of the machine. This, too, is being addressed by simpler, streamlined versions of the processors that are still fast yet provide a specific set of functions aimed at Mobile Computing. The result is a processor with the following characteristics:

- Ultra low-power consumption
- Small size
- Cool running
- Low cost.

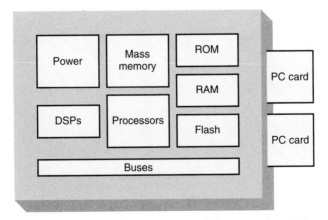

Figure B.4 The components of a mobile computing device.

Faster bus architectures are needed to handle the data generated by faster processors. To speed the data among the components of the device we need higher and higher performance buses. Without faster buses to match the faster processors, moving the data within the computer becomes a bottleneck, and the overall performance is reduced.

In this area, the winners are moving towards a distributed bus architecture with local buses carrying the "local" traffic and sharing a backbone bus. The backbone bus of choice is tending toward the ISA architecture. The trend is towards higher bandwidth and greater flexibility. Emerging distributed architecture such as the ISA bus combined with local buses is being chosen rather than 32 bit buses such as EISA.

DSPs are the cornerstone for multimedia. These hardware units are similar to engines that perform analog and digital processes with speed and efficiency. They process all the signals that start out as analog signals including speech, video, modem signals, and fax signals. In the area of recognition of speech and handwriting, DSPs are indispensable.

Longer running time and smaller lighter batteries are other key areas of development for mobile devices. In the last decade, the biggest hero had the most MHz, which translates to speed. These processors run at high temperatures and require lots of battery power. In this decade, the heroes combine speed with ultra-low power consumption as well as cool running. The trend is to move from 5 volts all the way down to A.5 volt by the end of the decade. Coupled with the drop in voltage, we will see more and more sophisticated power management features. At this time, power management techniques turn off different chips of the computer if they are not needed; in the future, power management systems will turn off parts of the chip when they are not required. In other words, power management will become more and more granular.

One of the keys to lower power and smaller size is small feature size. This is the size of the components on the chips. We expect to achieve 0.25 micron by the end of the decade as shown in Figure B.5.

More storage space for audio and video provides another dimension of growth for mobile computing devices. Disk drive performance has increased even faster than anticipated due to two

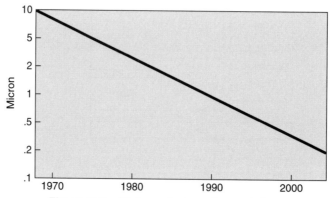

Figure B.5 Minimum feature size evolution.

new technologies: Magneto sensitive (MS) heads, and Partial Response Maximum Likelihood (PRML) technology. In addition, the rotational speeds of the platters where the data are stored is increasing from 3,600 revolutions per minute to 5,400 revolutions per minute and higher. In this area of storage, we expect 1 Gbyte to be generally available for Mobile Computing by the end of the decade on PCMCIA cards.

RAM is one of the cornerstones of sophisticated applications. It allows the computer to keep larger and larger amounts of data "in mind" as it processes it. Not having enough RAM would require the processor to "page" data in and out of mass memory. The growth of RAM is shown in Figure B.6.

This means that parts of a large application or file are actually "paged" into the hard disk when they are not immediately needed. The computer would need to do this in order to free up limited RAM space for it to perform its functions. When that part of the application or file is needed, the processor must take time to bring it back to RAM, and page another part of the application or file into the hard disk. This greatly slows down the operation of the overall computer. 16-Mbit chips are common now; 64-Mbit chips are beginning to appear on the market in volume; and 256-Mbit chips have been built in the lab and are functioning well at this time.

ROM holds the core functions of the computer. ROM maintains its memory when the power is turned off. In smaller computers such as PDAs, the ROM can hold not only the basic functions of the computer including its operating system but also some core applications such as telephone directory, appointment calendar, a small spreadsheet program, and a word processor. We expect ROM to reach a density of 256 Mbit per chip by the end of the decade.

Flash memory is the cousin of ROM. Usually housed in a PCMCIA card, it contains specific applications. Flash cards are experiencing the largest growth in the memory market. Because they can be plugged in and out by the user with ease, flash cards provide great flexibility. By holding different applications, they provide flexibility so that the same computer is able to address many different scenarios or even different vertical markets.

PCMCIA cards started out being for memory only as their name reflects. Now they provide all sorts of add-on functions. As we discussed above, ROM PCMCIA cards are called "flash

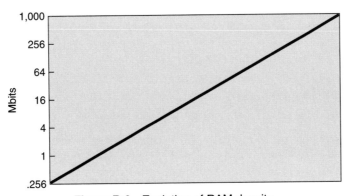

Figure B.6 Evolution of RAM density.

cards." Mass memory on a PCMCIA card is a low-profile rotating hard disk. Fax modems and Wireless LAN cards are now available in the PCMCIA form factor. These LAN cards provide over 1 Mbit per second data rate providing access from a portable computer or a PDA to a backbone LAN network such as Ethernet. Since a LAN is a private network, the user does not pay usage charges. If he were using a public network, such as a cellular network, he would have to.

PCMCIA positioning systems are available. These cards have a Global Positioning System (GPS) receiver on them. The receiver obtains signals from GPS satellites that allow the user to ascertain where he is to great accuracy. Using this information, he can acquire information on how to get to another location. Finally, service providers can use PCMCIA cards to provide vertical applications for specific market segments including public safety and real estate professionals. In summary, PCMCIA cards are providing:

- Memory cards
  - ROM
  - RAM
  - Mass memory
- Communications
  - Data/fax modems
  - LAN cards
- Vertical applications
  - Positioning systems
  - Public safety
  - Emergency disaster response
  - Real estate appraisals
  - Consumer guides.

How can a supplier achieve good economies of scale and at the same time serve the vertical market? The key is a customizable mobile computer that accepts PCMCIA cards with specific applications to give it the character of the vertical market segment that it is serving.

Mobile Operating Systems

This is the area highlighted in Figure B.7 that enables applications writers to develop applications with ease and without the undue burden of having to write complicated networking drivers.

Some examples of current mobile operating systems are:

- General Magic's Magic Cap
- Apple Newton operating system

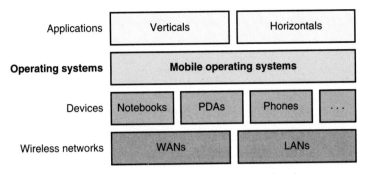

Figure B.7   Mobile operating systems level.

- Penpoint
- PenDOS
- GEOs.

   With a good mobile operating system, the applications writers can focus on the vertical or horizontal market they are serving. They do not have to hire and train networking experts to develop interface software to the different kinds of networks. Mobile operating systems simplify and speed the writing of applications.

   We hear a lot about software agents. These are software entities that act as macros. They take a simple user command such as found in the nearest Chinese restaurant and translate it into data retrieval queries, network access commands, and so forth. Agents are especially important in large complex networks such as the Internet. They are indispensable for tasks to find files of interest and other resources that may be on any one of thousands of hosts all over the world. We will see agents of all kinds being used in Mobile Computing to ease the user interface.

Market Forecasts

   In this section, we present some relative market forecasts not so much for their absolute value but rather to understand the comparable trends among different parts of the Mobile Computing, Mobile Data, and Wireless LAN markets. The mobile professional market is shown in Figure B.8.

   The first striking feature of Figure B.8 is that although the market for Mobile Data, mobile computers, and PDAs is quite large, it is small compared to the market for paging and cellular phones. This figure shows the number of users. If it showed total revenues instead, the difference would not be so dramatic.

   Next, we see that cellular has overtaken paging in terms of number of users. In terms of revenues, the acceleration of the cellular market is even more dramatic. The Mobile Data curve re-

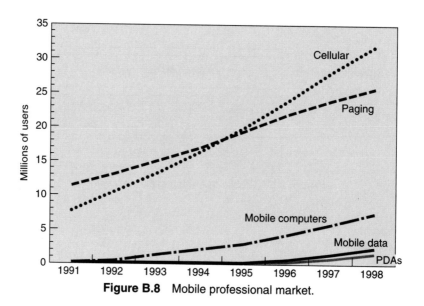

Figure B.8 Mobile professional market.

flects all Mobile Data adaptors in all types of devices including mobile computers, PDAs, cellular phones, and so on. The next curve is for mobile computers, and we all know how well that industry has been performing. Finally, the PDA market is shown.

The number of mobile computers with no networking, the number having Wireless WAN connectivity, and the ones having Wireless LAN connectivity are shown in Figure B.9.

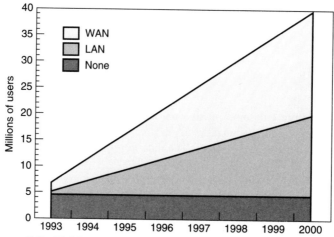

Figure B.9 Mobile computers with and without wireless connectivity.

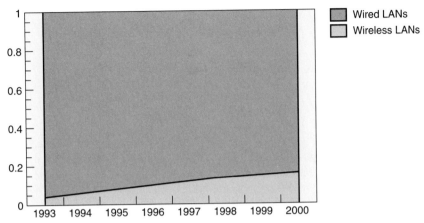

Figure B.10 Wireless LAN market comparet to wired LAN market.

Originally, the Wireless LAN market was considered part of the wired LAN market. Now we know that the wireless LAN market is a complement to the wired LAN market. Growth rates are greater than originally anticipated, and the unit prices are lower. Figure B.10 shows the percent of the LAN market that is wireless.

As shown, Wireless LANs by no means replace wired LANs. They will rise to about 20 percent of the market by the end of the decade. This prediction is sensitive to the price of the devices. The price of the devices can drop dramatically, if we have a viable standard that manufacturers can build chip sets to.

Finally, Figure B.11 shows the Wireless LAN market as a portion of all wireless data that includes both Wireless LANs, and Mobile Data.

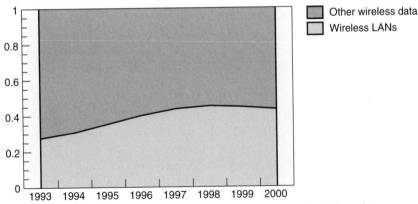

Figure B.11 Wireless LAN market compared to all wireless data.

As seen, the Wireless LAN market eventually garners about a 40 percent share of the market. The other 60 percent of mobile devices have Wireless WAN or Mobile Data connectivity.

Summary

In this Appendix we discussed two layers of Mobile Computing: The mobile computing devices layer and the mobile operating system layer. In the next chapter we discuss the applications layer. The rest of the book deals with the networking layer in detail. In this chapter, first we discussed Mobile Computing devices that are carryable, pocketable, and wearable. We showed that the potential volume for the smaller size devices can be much larger than for the bigger, more expensive devices, and that these smaller devices benefit most from mobility functions.

Focusing on pocketable devices, we discussed the heritage of the different factions of the industry that are introducing mobile devices including computer companies and telephony companies. However, the character of these devices and their names are different. It is exciting to watch the evolution of these devices as more and more functionality is added to them. We discussed the cost of the devices and their appeal to the vertical markets, the horizontal professional market, and the horizontal consumer market.

Next, we explored the evolution of the technologies underlying Mobile Computing devices including: processors, buses, power subsystems, DSPs, and memory systems including ROM, RAM, flash, and PC cards. We showed the evolution in the technology for each of these components. We saw the emphasis for mobile devices in their ultra-low power consumption, small size, cool running, low cost, and their ability to handle speech, handwriting, pen strokes, and perhaps eventually video. DSPs play an especially important role here.

We discussed the importance of a good mobile operating system. Operating system providers including Microsoft are providing these mobile capabilities as part of the core operating system. Having a good mobile operating system speeds the emergence of good applications that are key to the growth of the industry.

Finally, we presented some relative market forecasts. The key points that emerged are that the Mobile Computing, Mobile Data, and Wireless LAN markets are very significant, but they are small when compared with the market for cellular and paging in terms of number of users. Next, we noted that the majority of Mobile Computing devices will have either a Mobile Data connection, a Wireless LAN connection, or both. We showed that the Wireless LAN market grows to about 20 percent of the total LAN market, and that the Wireless LAN market peaks at about 40 percent of the total Wireless Data market that includes both Mobile Data and Wireless LANs.

APPENDIX C
List of GSM Technical Specifications

This appendix lists the technical specifications of the GSM Standard. The number of pages in each specification is also shown to give an idea of the level of detail in each specification. The total number of pages is 5,230.

01 Series: General

- 01.04: Vocabulary in a GSM PLMN, 51 pages
- 01.06: Service implementation phases and possible further phases in the GSM PLMN, 3 pages

02 Series: Service Aspects

- 02.01: Principles of telecommunication services supported by a GSM PLMN, 18 pages
- 02.02: Bearer services supported by a GSM PLMN, 38 pages
- 02.03: Teleservices supported by a GSM PLMN, 23 pages
- 02.04: General information on supplementary services, 18 pages
- 02.05: Simultaneous and alternate use of services, 3 pages
- 02.06: Types of mobile stations, 4 pages
- 02.07: Mobile station features, 15 pages

- 02.09: Security aspects, 8 pages
- 02.10: Provision of telecommunications services
- 02.11: Service accessibility, 7 pages
- 02.12: Licensing, 2 pages
- 02.13: Subscription to the services of a GSM PLMN
- 02.14: Service directory, 2 pages
- 02.15: Circulation of mobile stations, 2 pages
- 02.16: International MS equipment identities, 5 pages
- 02.17: Subscriber identity modules, functional characteristics, 11 pages
- 02.20: Collection charges, 11 pages
- 02.30: Man-machine interface of the mobile station, 18 pages
- 02.40: Procedures for call progress indications, 6 pages
- 02.82: Call offering supplementary services, 60 pages
- 02.88: Call restriction supplementary services, 18 pages
- 02.81: Number identification supplementary service
- 02.83: Call completion supplementary service
- 02.84: Multiparty supplementary service
- 02.85: Community of interest supplementary service
- 02.86: Charging supplementary service
- 02.87: Additional information transfer supplementary service

03 Series: Network Aspects

- 03.01: Network functions, 10 pages
- 03.02: Network architecture, 17 pages
- 03.03: Numbering, addressing, and identification, 14 pages
- 03.04: Signaling requirements relating to routing of calls to mobile subscribers, 11 pages
- 03.05: Technical performance objectives, 23 pages
- 03.07: Restoration procedures, 11 pages
- 03.08: Organization of subscriber data, 18 pages
- 03.09: Handover procedures, 38 pages

- 03.10: GSM PLMN connection types, 39 pages
- 03.11: Technical realization of supplementary services—general aspects, 14 pages
- 03.12: Location registration procedures, 9 pages
- 03.13: Discontinuous reception in the GSM system, 4 pages
- 03.14: Support of DTMF via the GSM system, 8 pages
- 03.20: Security related network functions, 44 pages
- 03.40: Technical realization of the Short Message Service point to point, 100 pages
- 03.41: Technical realization of the Short Message service cell broadcast, 7 pages
- 03.43: Technical realization of the videotex, 11 pages
- 03.44: Support of teletext in a GSM PLMN, 16 pages
- 03.45: Technical realization of the facsimile group 3 service—transparent, 37 pages
- 03.46: Technical realization of the facsimile group 3 service—nontransparent, 42 pages
- 03.50: Transmission planning aspects of the speech service in the GSM PLMN system, 30 pages
- 03.70: Routing of calls to and from PDNs, 12 pages
- 03.82: Technical realization of the call offering supplementary services, 982 pages
- 03.88: Technical realization of the call restriction supplementary services, 29 pages

04 Series: MS-BS Interfaces and Protocols

- 04.01: MS-BSS interface = General aspects and principles, 7 pages
- 04.02: GSM PLMN access reference configurations, 6 pages
- 04.03: MS-BSS interface—Channel structures and access, 9 pages
- 04.04: MS-BSS Layer 1—General requirements, 19 pages
- 04.05: MS-BSS data link layer—General aspects, 24 pages
- 04.06: MS-BSS data link layer—Specification, 83 pages
- 04.07: Mobile radio interface signaling layer 3—General aspects, 62 pages

- 04.08: Mobile radio interface layer 3—Specification, 446 pages
- 04.10: Mobile radio interface layer 3—Supplementary services specification—General aspects, 22 pages
- 04.11: Point-to-point short message service support on mobile radio interface, 72 pages
- 04.12: Cell broadcast short message service support on mobile radio interface, 4 pages
- 04.21: Rate adaptation on MS-BSS interface, 12 pages
- 04.22: Radio link protocol for data and telematic services on the MS-BSS interface, 59 pages
- 04.80: Mobile radio interface layer 3—Supplementary services specification—Formats and coding, 38 pages
- 04.82: Mobile radio interface layer 3—Call offering supplementary services specification, 34 pages
- 04.83: Mobile radio interface layer 3—Call restriction supplementary services specification, 12 pages

05 Series: Physical Layer on the Radio Path

- 05.01: Physical layer on the radio path—General description, 11 pages
- 05.02: Multiplexing and multiple access on the radio path, 36 pages
- 05.03: Channel coding, 22 pages
- 05.04: Modulation, 3 pages
- 05.05: Radio transmission and reception, 19 pages
- 05.08: Radio subsystem link control, 38 pages
- 05.10: Radio subsystem synchronization, 6 pages

06 Series: Speech Coding Specification

- 06.01: Speech processing functions—General description, 8 pages
- 06.10: GSM full-rate speech transcoding, 93 pages

- 06.11: Substitution and muting of lost frames for full rate speech traffic channels, 5 pages
- 06.12: Comfort noise aspects for full-rate speech traffic channels, 6 pages
- 06.31: Discontinuous transmission for full-rate speech traffic channels, 13 pages
- 06.32: Voice activity detection, 37 pages

07 Series: Terminal Adaptors for Mobile Stations

- 07.01: General on terminal adaptation functions for MSs, 49 pages
- 07.04: Terminal adaptation functions for services using asynchronous bearer capabilities, 17 pages
- 07.03: Terminal adaptation functions for services using synchronous bearer capabilities, 36 pages

08 Series: BS to MSC Interfaces

- 08.01: General aspects on the BSS-MSC interface, 5 pages
- 08.02: BSS-MSC interface—Interface principles, 17 pages
- 08.04: BSS-MSC layer 1 specification, 2 pages
- 08.06: Signaling transport mechanism specification for the BSS-MSC interface, 29 pages
- 08.08: BSS-MSC layer 3 specification, 92 pages
- 08.20: Rate adaptation on the BSS-MSC interface, 5 pages
- 08.51: BSC-BTS interface, general aspects, 4 pages
- 08.52: BSC-BTS interface principles, 15 pages
- 08.54: BSC-TRX layer 1—Structure of physical circuits, 3 pages
- 08.56: BSC-BTS layer 2 specification, 11 pages
- 08.58: BSC-BTS layer 3 specification, 80 pages
- 08.59: BSC-BTS O&M signaling transport, 6 pages
- 08.60: In-band control of remote transcoders and rate adaptors, 29 pages

09 Series: Network Interworking

- 09.01: General network interworking scenarios, 8 pages
- 09.02: Mobile application part specification, 507 pages
- 09.03: Requirements on interworking between the ISDN or PSTN and the PLMN, 6 pages
- 09.04: Interworking between the PLMN and the CSPDN, 12 pages
- 09.05: Interworking between the PLMN and OSODN for PAD access, 19 pages
- 09.07: General requirements on interworking between the PLMN and the ISN or PSTN, 53 pages
- 09.09: Detailed signaling interworking within the PLMN and with the PSTN/ISDN, 36 pages
- 09.10: Information element mapping between MS-BSS/BSS-MSC signaling procedures and MAP, 16 pages
- 09.11: Signaling interworking for supplementary services, 9 pages

11 Series: Equipment and Type Approval Specification

- 11.10: Mobile station conformity specifications, 523 pages
- 11.11: Specification of the SIM-ME interface, 131 pages
- 11.20: The GSM base station system—equipment specification, 423 pages
- 11.30: Mobile services switching center, 55 pages
- 11.31: Home location register specification, 9 pages
- 11.32: Visitor location register specification, 13 pages
- 11.40: System simulator specification, 46 pages

12 Series: Operation and Maintenance

- 12.00: Objectives and structure of network management, 51 pages
- 12.01: Common aspects of GSM network management, 69 pages

- 12.02: Subscriber, mobile equipment, and services data administration, 17 pages
- 12.03: Security management, 16 pages
- 12.04: Performance data measurements, 45 pages
- 12.05: Subscriber-related event and call data, 18 pages
- 12.06: GSM network change control, 27 pages
- 12.07: Operations and performance management, 61 pages
- 12.10: Maintenance provisions for operational integrity of MSs, 6 pages
- 12.11: Maintenance of the base station subsystem, 39 pages
- 12.13: Maintenance of the mobile services switching center, 10 pages
- 12.14: Maintenance of location registers, 9 pages
- 12.20: Network management procedures and messages, 342 pages
- 12.21: Network management procedures and messages on the Abis interface, 83 pages

List of Wireless Networking Companies

APPENDIX D

A

Advanced Wireless Communications, Inc.
435 Indio Way
Sunnyvale, CA 94086
(408) 736-8833

Alcatel Network Systems
12245 North Alma Road
Richardson, TX 75081
(214) 996-5000

Advantis
3401 West Drive
Martin Luther King, Jr. Boulevard
Tampa, FL 33607
(813) 878-4207

Air Communications, Inc.
274 San Geronimo Way
Sunnyvale, CA 94086
(408) 749-9883

AirTouch Teletrac
7391 Lincoln Way
Garden Grove, CA 92641
(714) 890-7626

ALPS Electric, Inc.
3553 North First Street
San Jose, CA 95134
(408) 432-6544

American Mobile Satellite Corp.
10802 Parkridge Boulevard
Reston, VA 22091
(703) 758-6000

American Personal Communication
1025 Connecticut Avenue
Washington, D.C. 20036
(202) 296-0005

Ameritech Mobile Communications
2000 West Ameritech Center Drive
Hoffman Estates, IL 60195
(708) 234-9700

Apple Computer
2025 Mariani Avenue
Cupertino, CA 95014
(408) 974-6790

ARDIS
300 Knightsbridge Parkway
Lincolnshire, IL 60069
(708) 013-1215

Arther D. Little, Inc.
Acorn Park
Cambridge, MA 02140
(617) 864-5770

AT&T
67 Whippany Road
Whippany, NJ 07981
(201) 386-7765

AT&T Network Systems
111 Madison Avenue
Morristown, NJ 07962
(201) 606-4060

AT&T Paradyne
8545 126th Avenue
Largo, FL 34649
(813) 530-8167

B

Bell Atlantic Mobile Systems
180 Washington Valley Road
Bedminster, NJ 07921
(908) 306-7583

Bellcore
290 West Mt. Pleasant Avenue
Livingston, NJ 07039
(800) 523-2673

Bell South Cellular
1100 Peachtree Street
Atlanta, GA 30309
(404) 249-5000

BIS Strategic Decisions
One Longwater Circle
Norwalk, MA 02061
(617) 982-9500

BT, Ltd.
Annandale House
1 Hanworth Road
Surrey 44 932 765 766

BT North America
2560 North First Street
San Jose, CA 95161
(800) 872-7654

C

California Microwave, Inc.
985 Almandor Avenue
Sunnyvale, CA 94086
(408) 732-4000

Casio, Inc.
570 Mt. Pleasant Avenue
Dover, NJ 07801
(201) 361-5400

Cellular One
5001 LBJ Freeway
Dallas, TX 75244
(214) 443-9901

Cincinnati Microwave, Inc.
One Microwave Plaza
Cincinnati, OH 45249
(513) 489-5400

C. Itoh & Co.
251 Kita Aoyama
Tokyo 107, Japan
03 3497 3186

Claris Corp.
201 Patrick Henry Drive
Santa Clara, CA 95052
(408) 987-4000

Communications Industry Association of Japan
92 Ohtemachi, 1 chome
Chiyoda ku, Tokyo, Japan
03 3231 3156

CTIA
1250 Connecticut Avenue
Washington, D.C. 20036
(202) 785-0081

Cylink
310 North Mary Avenue
Sunnyvale, CA 94087
(408) 735-5817

D

Dauphin Technology, Inc.
377 East Butterfield Street
Lombard, IL 60148
(708) 971-3400

Digital Microwave Corp.
170 Rose Orchard Way
San Jose, CA 95134
(408) 973-0777

Digital Ocean, Inc.
11206 Thompson Avenue
Lenexa, KS 66219
(913) 888-3380

E

Electronic Industries Ass'n.
2500 Wilson Boulevard
Arlington, VA 22209
(703) 524-5550

EMI Communications Corp.
PO Box 4872
Syracuse, NY 13221
(315) 433-0022

E-Plus Mobilfunk
Hans Guenther Sohl Strasse 1
4000 Düsseldorf 1
49 211 967 7590

Ericsson Business Communications, Inc.
5757 Plaza Drive
Cypress, CA 90630
(714) 236-6500

Ericsson Radio Systems, Inc.
740 East Campbell Road
Richardson, TX 75081
(214) 238-3222

Ex Mahnica, Inc.
45 East 89th Street
New York, NY 10128
(718) 965-0309

F

Federal Communications Commission
1919 M. Street, NW
Washington, D.C. 20055
(202) 632 7557
  Office of Engineering and Technology
  (202) 653-8117
  Spectrum Allocations
  (202) 652-8108
  Common Carrier Bureau
  (202) 634-7058

Frost & Sullivan Int.
4 Grosvenor Gardens
London, UK
071 730 3438

Fujitsu Personal Systems, Inc.
5200 Patrick Henry Drive
Santa Clara, CA 95054
(408) 982-9500

G

Gandlaf Mobile Systems, Inc.
2 Gurdwara Road
Nepean, Ontario, Canada
(613) 723-6500

GEO Systems
227 Granite Run Drive
Lancaster, PA 17601
(717) 293-7500

GeoWorks
2150 Shattuck Avenue
Berkeley, CA 94704
(510) 644-0883

GPS International Ass'n.
206 East College Street
Grapevine, TX 76051
(800) 269-1073

Granite Communications, Inc.
9 Townsend West
Nashua, NH 03063
(603) 881-8666

GTE Mobile Communications
245 Perimeter Center Parkway
Atlanta, GA 30348
(404) 391-8386

GTE PCS Group
600 North West Shore Boulevard
Tampa, FL 33609
(813) 282-6154

H

Hewlett Packard Co.
5301 Stevens Creek Boulevard
Santa Clara, CA 95052

Hong Kong Telecom, Ltd.
City Plaza Three
Hong Kong
852 803 8231

Hutchison Paging, Ltd.
Manlong House
911 615 Nathan Road
Kowloon
Hong Kong
(852) 710-6828

I

IBM Personal Computer Co.
1000 NW 51st Street
Boca Raton, FL 33432
(407) 443-2000

IEEE
445 Hoes Lane
Piscataway, NJ 08855
(908) 981-0060

InfraLAN Technologies, Inc.
12 Craig Road
Acton, MA 01720
(508) 266-1500

Iridium, Inc.
1350 I Street
Washington, D.C. 20005
(202) 371-6889

J

Japan Ministry of Posts and Telecommunications
132 Kasumigaseki, Chiyoda ku
Tokyo 10090, Japan
03 3504 4086

Japan R&D Center for Radio Systems
1516 Toranoman
Minato ku Tokyo 105, Japan
03 3592 1101

K

Kenwood USA Corp.
2201 East Dominiquez Street
Long Beach, CA 90810
(310) 639-9000

L

Link Resources Corp.
79 Fifth Avenue
New York, NY 10003
(212) 627-1500

Loral Aerospace Corp.
7375 Executive Place
Seabrook, MD 20706
(301) 805-0591

M

Matra Marconi Space
7 rue Hermes
31520 Ramonvill Street
Agne, France
33 61 750565

McCaw Cellular Communications, Inc.
P.O. Box 97060
Kirkland, WA 98083
(206) 827-4500

Megahertz Corp.
4505 South Wasatch Boulevard
Salt Lake City, UT 84124

Mercury Communications, Ltd.
90 Long Acre
London 2C239N
44 71 836 2449

Metricom, Inc.
980 University Avenue
Los Gatos, CA 95030
(408) 299-8200

Motorola Cellular Infrastructure Group
1501 West Shure Drive
Arlington Heights, IL 60004
(708) 632-5000

Motorola/EMBARC
1500 NW 22d Avenue
Boyton Beach, FL 33426
(407) 364-2000

Motorola, Inc.
Cellular Subscriber Group
600 North U.S. Highway 45
Libertyville, IL 60048
(708) 523-5000

N

NTIA
U.S. Department of Commerce
Washington, D.C. 20230
(202) 377-1866

NEC America
Mobile Radio Division
383 Omni Drive
Richardson, TX 75080
(800) 421-2141

NEXTEL Communications
201 Route 17 North
Rutherford, NJ 07070
(201) 438-1400

Nokia Mobile Phones
2300 Tall Pines Drive
Largo, FL 34741
(813) 536-4443

Northern Telecom
2221 Lakeside Boulevard
Richardson, TX 75208
(214) 684-8821

NovAtel Communications, Ltd.
6732 8th Street
Calgary, Alberta
Canada T2E8M4
(403) 295-4949

NYNEX Mobile Communications Co.
2000 Corporate Drive
Orangeburg, NY 10962
(914) 365-7712

O

Oki Telecom
437 Old Peachtree Road
Suwanee, GA 30174
(404) 995-9800

Omnipoint Corp.
7150 Campus Drive
Colorado Springs, CO 80920
(719) 591-0823

P

Pacific Communications Sciences, Inc.
10075 Barnes Canyon Road
San Diego, CA 92121
(619) 535-9500

PacTel Corp.
2999 Oak Road
Walnut Creek, CA 94596
(510) 210-3645

PCMCIA
1030 East Duane Avenue
Sunnyvale, CA 94086
(408) 720-0107

Photonics Corp.
2940 North First Street
San Jose, CA 95134
(408) 955-7930

Pinpoint Communications, Inc.
12750 Merit Drive
Dallas, TX 75251
(214) 789-8900

Proxim, Inc.
295 North Bernardo Avenue
Mountain View, CA 94043
(415) 960-1630

Q

Qualcomm, Inc.
6455 Lus Boulevard
San Diego, CA 92121
(619) 587-1121

R

Racoteck, Inc.
7401 Metro Boulevard
Minneapolis, MN 55439
(612) 832-9800

Radiance Communications, Inc.
2338A Walsh Avenue
Santa Clara, CA 95051
(408) 980-5380

RadioMail Corp.
2600 Campus Drive
San Mateo, CA 94403
(415) 286-7800

RAM Mobile Data
10 Woodbridge Center
Woodbridge, NJ 07095
(908) 602-5603

S

SkyTel Corp.
1350 I Street NW
Washington, D.C. 20005
(202) 408-7444

Southwestern Bell Mobile Systems
18111 Preston Road
Dallas, TX 75252
(214) 613-0000

SpectraLink Corp.
1650 38th Street
Boulder, CO 80301
(303) 440-5330

Sprint Cellular
8725 West Higgins Road
Chicago, IL 60631
(312) 399-2828

Stanford Telecommunications, Inc.
2421 Mission College Boulevard
Santa Clara, CA 95056
(408) 746-1010

Symbol Technologies, Inc.
46 Wilbur Place
Bohemia, NY 11716
(800) SCAN-234

T

Technologic Partners
419 Park Avenue
New York, NY 10016
(212) 696-9330

Telecom Denmark
Telegrade 2
DK 2630 Hoje Taastrup
AS reg. nr. 193312
45 42 52 9111

Telecommunications Industry Association
2001 Pennsylvania Avenue
Washington, D.C. 20006
(202) 457-8737

Teledesic Corp.
16161 Ventura Boulevard
Encino, CA 91436
(818) 907-1302

Traveling Software
19802 North Creek Parkway
Bethel, WA 98011

U

United States Telephone Ass'n.
1401 H. Street, NW
Washington, D.C. 20005
(202) 326-7300

US West
3350 161st Avenue
Bellevue, WA 98008
(206) 747-4900

W

WaveLAN Products
1700 South Patterson Boulevard
Dayton OH 45479
(800) 255-5627

Windata
10 Bearfoot Road
Northboro, MA 01532
(508) 393-3330

X

Xircom
26025 Murearu Road
Calabasas, CA 91360
(818) 878-6409

Y

Yankee Group
200 Portland Street
Cambridge, MA 02114

Z

Zenith Data Systems
2150 East Lake Cook Road
Buffalo Grove, IL 60089
(800) 553-0331

Glossary

A

ACC:	Area Communications Controller
ACK:	ACKnowledgment
ADPCM:	Adaptive Delta Pulse Code Modulation
ALOHA:	(Hello and Good-bye in Hawaiian!) Not an acronym
AM:	Amplitude Modulation
AMPS:	Advanced Mobile Phone Service

B

BTA:	Basic Trading Area

C

CAI:	Common Air Interface
CDM:	Code Division Multiplexing
CDPD:	Cellular Digital Packet Data
CEPT:	Conference of European PTs
CDMA:	Code Division Multiple Access

CSMA:	Carrier Sense Multiple Access
CSMA/CD:	Carrier Sense Multiple Access/Collision Detection
CT:	Cordless Telephone

D

DCS:	Digital Communications Services
DECT:	Digital European Cordless Telephone
Demux:	Demultiplexer
DES:	Data Encryption Standard
DQPSK:	Differential Quadrature Phase Shift Keying
DS:	Direct Sequence
DSP:	Digital Signal Processor
DSRR:	Digital Short Range Radio

E

ECMA:	European Computer Manufacturers Association
EDC:	Error Detection and Correction
EEC:	European Economic Community
EIA:	Electronics Industry Association
ERMES:	European Radio Message Service
ET:	Extra Terrestrial! Emerging Technologies
ETSI:	European Telecommunications Standards Institute

F

FCC:	Federal Communications Commission
FDD:	Frequency Division Duplexing
FDM:	Frequency Division Multiplexing

FDMA: Frequency Division Multiple Access

FH: Frequency Hopping

FSK: Frequency Shift Keying

G

GFSK: Gaussian Frequency Shift Keying

GMSK: Gaussian Minimum Shift Keying

GPS: Global Positioning System

GR: Gamma Rays

GSM: Groupe Speciale Mobile

H

HH: Hand-Held

HLR: Home Locations Register

I

IA: Information Appliance

IEEE: Institute of Electrical and Electronics Engineers

IEIE: Institute of Electronic and Information Engineers

ISDN: Integrated Services Digital Network

ISI: Inter Symbol Interference

ISM: Industrial Scientific and Medical

J

JDC: Japanese Digital Cellular

JTC: Joint Technical Committee

L

LAN: Local Area Network

LAP: Link Access Protocol

LEO: Low Earth Orbit

LLC: Logical Link Control (layer)

M

MAC: Medium Access Control (layer)

MPT: Ministry of Public Telecommunications

Mux: Multiplexer

N

NMT: Nordic Mobile Telecommunications

NoR: Notice of Rulemaking

NPRM: Notice of Proposed Rulemaking

ns: nanosecond = 10^{-9} second

P

PAMR: Public Access Mobile Radio

PBX: Private Branch eXchange

PCMCIA: Personal Computer Memory Card Industry Association

PCN: Personal Communications Network

PCS: Personal Communications Services

PDA: Personal Digital Assistant

PHY: PHYsical (layer)

PM: Phase Modulation

PMR: Private Mobile Radio

POCSAG: Post Office Code Standardization Advisory Group

POS: Point of Sale

PSK: Phase Shift Keying

PSTN: Public Switched Telephone Network

Q

QAM: Quadrature Amplitude Modulation

QPSK: Quadrature Phase Shift Keying

R

RELP: Residually Excited Linear Predictive

RES: Radio Equipment and Systems

RSA: Rivest/Shamir/Adelman

RX: Receiver

S

SIM: Subscriber Identity Module

SMR: Specialized Mobile Radio

SMS: Short Message Service

SS: Spread Spectrum

T

Tab: Not a TLA!

TACS: Total Access Communications System

TCP/IP: Transmission Control Protocol/Internet Protocol

TDD: Time Division Duplexing

TDM: Time Division Multiplexing

TDMA: Time Division Multiple Access

TLA: Three Letter Acronym

TX: Transmitter

U

UPT: Universal Personal Telecommunications

μs: microsecond = 10^{-6} second

USDC: US Digital Cellular

V

VAN: Value Added Network

W

WAN: Wide Area Network

WARC: World Administrative Radio Conference.

About the Author

Dr. Dayem is principal and founder of Altamont Research, a market and technology analysis firm focusing on Wireless Networking in Cupertino, CA, U.S. He is a pioneer in the field of Wireless Networking. He received degrees in physics and engineering from Cornell and Stanford. At Bell Labs he was instrumental in designing private network services and at Apple, he spearheaded the Wireless Networking effort.

Dr. Dayem has presented seminars and chaired sessions on Wireless Networking in the United States, Europe, and Asia—most recently at NetWorld+Interop, Frost & Sullivan, Institute for International Research, Wireless Datacom, and Mobile Solutions. His consulting clients include computer manufacturers, chip manufacturers, Mobile Data companies, Wireless LAN companies, retail chains including Sears, and other end users such as Walt Disney.

At Apple, Dr. Dayem was a key member of a team addressing the user needs, technology options, and the standards and regulatory issues leading to a Wireless Networking strategy for the company. He led the software development of local area network connectivity products for Macintosh and directed the Campus Network Development Department in developing and implementing a voice and local area network for Apple as well. The network serves as the foundation for critical applications: namely, electronic mail, directory, and growing multimedia applications.

At Northern Telecom, he was director of product marketing through Integrated Office Systems. He established a major accounts technical marketing program. His responsibilities included numerous discussions with customers as well as applications studies. The product line included network services, PBXs, packet switches, and transmission systems.

He worked ten years at Bell Telephone Labs where he made key contributions in areas of private networks, microwave radio, and satellite communication. In particular, his contributions included: combined circuit and packet switching for multimedia applications and equalization in the presence of deep fading that were instrumental in tripling the capacity of microwave radio channels in the Bell System.

Dr. Dayem obtained a BS with distinction in Physics from Cornell University, an MS in Physics/EE from Stanford University, and a PhD in Physics/EE from the University of Pennsylvania. He also obtained an MBA as a member of the charter class of the San Jose State MBA program at Apple Computer. He is a member of Tau Beta Pi and was president of Phi Sigma Kappa.

INDEX